DATE DUE

NO 27 96		
DE 4 98		
DE 18 99		
JE 6 01		
DE 21 02		
JE 5 03		
JE 9 03		
DE 17 04		

DEMCO 38-296

The Voice of the People

The Voice of the People

PUBLIC OPINION AND DEMOCRACY

James S. Fishkin

Yale University Press   New Haven and London

Designed by Sonia L. Scanlon.

Set in Times Roman type by Marathon Typography Services,
Inc., Durham, North Carolina.

Printed in the United States of America by Vail-Ballou Press,
Binghamton, New York.

Fishkin, James S.

The voice of the people : public opinion and democracy /
James S. Fishkin.

p.   cm.

Includes bibliographical references and index.

ISBN 0-300-06556-6 (alk. paper)

1. Political participation—United States.   2. Democracy
—United States.   3. Public opinion—United States.

I. Title.

JK1764.F53 1995

323'.042'0973—dc20   95–34620

CIP

A catalogue record for this book is available from the British
Library.

The paper in this book meets the guidelines for permanence
and durability of the Committee on Production Guidelines for
Book Longevity of the Council on Library Resources.

10   9   8   7   6   5   4   3   2   1

CONTENTS

ACKNOWLEDGMENTS

This book is the fruit of many collaborations and influences. The prime intellectual influences are probably from Robert Dahl and Peter Laslett—Dahl turned me to democratic theory and Laslett's striking early essay "The Face-to-Face Society" stimulated my thinking about how to adapt the democracy of the small group to the nation-state.

In addition, the process of attempting to develop the deliberative poll in two countries has taught me a great deal. My colleagues in British television, particularly David Lloyd, Fiona Chesterton, and Julie Hall of Channel 4 and Charles Tremayne, Dorothy Byrne, and Christine Ruth of Granada Television, have been invaluable. In the United States, I would particularly like to thank Dan Werner of the MacNeil/Lehrer NewsHour, Ed Fouhy of the Pew Center for Civic Journalism, and Dick Richter of WETA. The superb leadership Ervin Duggan is lending to PBS has made this project possible, while the able work of John Hollar, also at PBS, has been invaluable. I would also like to thank John Gibbons at Freddie Mac for having the insight to support the project at the crucial moment.

Roger Jowell and Becky Gray at Social and Community Planning Research (SCPR), Bob Luskin at the University of Texas and Norman Bradburn at the National Opinion Research Center (NORC) have been key in bringing the deliberative poll to realization. I am also grateful to Phil Converse for agreeing to head the Technical Review Committee that will supervise some important aspects of the effort in the United States.

The greatest source of energy and enthusiasm for the entire project has been Charly Walker. It could not have happened without him and without the many distinguished members of the advisory board he and Newton Minow put together. Many colleagues at the University of Texas have also been of great help, particularly Jeff Tulis, Sandy Levinson, and Dean Burnham in the department of government, Thomas Seung in the department of philosophy, and Barbara Jordan and Elspeth Rostow in the Lyndon Baines Johnson School of Public Affairs. My former colleague in communications, Kathleen Jamieson, continues to give invaluable advice. Finally, Shelley Fisher Fishkin and Milton Fisher have helped in more ways than I can begin to mention.

John Janssen has been a superb research assistant, and thanks are also due to Suzanne Colwell and Stephanie Galvan.

I have benefited greatly from my association with High Road Productions, for whom I have been an adviser on their series *The American Promise*. I would like to thank Denny Crimmins and Deborah Hudson for their help and for many useful suggestions.

I also wish to thank my many friends at the Yale University Press, particularly my editor, John Covell, and Tina Weiner, the associate director of the Press. They saw the role this book could play in the larger project, and they did not hesitate to make it happen in time.

The Voice of the People

1

INTRODUCTION

MAGIC TOWN

There is a classic Jimmy Stewart movie, *Magic Town,* about "Grand-view," a small town in the Midwest that is an exact statistical micro-cosm of the United States, a place where the citizens' opinions match perfectly with Gallup polls of the entire nation.[1] A pollster (Jimmy Stewart), secretly uses surveys from this "mathematical miracle" as a shortcut to predicting public opinion. Instead of collecting a national sample, he can more quickly and cheaply collect surveys from this single small town. The character played by Jane Wyman, a newspaper editor, finds out what is going on and publishes her discovery. As a re-sult the national media descend upon the town, which becomes, overnight, "the public opinion capital of the U.S." The citizens of Grandview become self-conscious because they are now "the perfect barometer of national opinion." They begin to feel a heavy responsi-bility, knowing that what they say will be listened to throughout the world. They arrange to collect their own survey, "The Official Grand-view Poll," but with the proviso that "reference libraries" be provided at every polling booth. Because the issues are important, they believe people should be informed.

With this new sense of responsibility, and their heightened interest in the issues, the townspeople's views soon diverge from those of the rest of the country. The climax comes when the town announces the result that 79 percent of them would be willing to "vote for a woman for president"! This is taken as such a preposterous departure from conventional opinion that they become a source of national ridicule. "The little town that has always been right turned out to be ridiculously wrong. People are beginning to wonder where Grandview is. Certainly it can't be in the United States." Comics start to use the explanation "He's from Grandview" as the punchline in jokes, to explain apparent idiocy.

Yet which opinions are more worth listening to? The conventional opinion of the time, offered in response to questions from the Gallup poll, that people should not support a woman for president, or the very different view the citizens of Grandview finally came to, when they thought their opinions would actually matter, and after they had had a chance to reexamine their prejudices and preconceptions? Those considered judgments were, indeed, unrepresentative of the views of the rest of the country. But then again, the rest of the country had not really thought much about the question.

Obviously, public opinion polls of the standard kind give us a snapshot of what the country is *actually* thinking. They are a valuable means of telling both the country and its political leaders about the current state of mass opinion. For that purpose, the new opinions of the Grandview citizens became worthless, just as the Jimmy Stewart character had said they would, once word got out. But for other purposes, particularly for finding a public voice worth listening to, the final views of Grandview offer a useful supplement to the vagaries of an inattentive public. There is a kind of recommending force to the new opinions at Grandview: this is what a microcosm of the country thinks about an issue once it has had a better chance to focus on it, to discuss it, and to reexamine shared preconceptions. Perhaps this is what the entire country, not just the microcosm, *would* think about the issue if it focused on it in a more sustained way.

Grandview symbolizes a central problem: when can a microcosm, or some other small *part* of the country, speak for the whole, speak for the entire citizenry and its interests? Polls offer one kind of microcosm, a statistical sample in which each citizen has an equal, random chance of participating. With random sampling we can closely approximate the views of the entire country without having to ask everyone. In fact, we need ask only a tiny fraction, provided it is properly selected.

In addition to such scientific samples, there are any number of *self*-selected groups that *seem* to speak for the people—from the voices on radio or television call-in shows, to the letters and faxes that pour into congressional offices, to the people who show up at campaign rallies or public meetings. Such groups may think they speak for everyone, but they are far more likely to speak merely for themselves. They offer contested and controversial representations of public opinion—representations that must be viewed through the prism of their interests in putting themselves forward. The same point applies, of course, to officeholders, media commentators, and pundits, who also presume, on almost a daily basis, to speak for the people. These people have interests and positions to maintain. Yes, in some sense they speak for the people, but the public has learned that such people also speak for themselves.

There is a fancy name for taking the part for the whole—*synecdoche*.[2] It is a form of representation that occurs regularly in politics, which is, after all, a process of allowing a part to stand for, or re-present, the whole. An elected Congress, the president, even the voters in a referendum (at the state level)—these all consist of parts of the people who are offered as speaking for all the people. Even opinion polls are mechanisms whereby statistical samples of the people can speak for everyone. Less convincingly, the self-selected studio audience in a televised "town meeting" will *seem* to speak for the people, but it is also a mere representation. On any given issue, there will be many parts available simultaneously to speak for the whole, each part purporting to speak authoritatively.

Accepting that there are many portions of the people who purport to speak *for* everyone, can we find conditions when all the people can speak without requiring surrogates, conditions where the whole can, in some sense, *speak for itself?* Even if we were to ask everyone what they thought about an issue, we would still be offering a representation, a picture, of public opinion. That opinion would have been formed under certain conditions, and those conditions may be far from favorable for the public being able to form a reasonable opinion, or even any coherent opinion at all. Representation comes from taking a part for the whole but it also comes from taking what the people seem to be saying at a snapshot in time—under one set of conditions—as a representation of what they *really* think. As we shall see, they may not "really" be thinking much at all. In a broad sense, there will always be conflicting representations of public opinion, but there will also be conditions, which we can distinguish, under which the voices of the people are more, or less, worth listening to.

Conflicting representations of public opinion are inescapable. Even a decisive election will yield different interpretations of the mandate, via alternative exit polls, contradictory views of commentators and pundits, surveys before and after the fact, interpretations of what different portions of the public might wish, and "spin-doctoring" by political actors with disparate interests at stake in the view of current history that comes to be accepted.

In spite of these conflicts, there is one simple answer to the question—When can the people *best* speak for themselves?—that runs through the history of democratic experimentation: The public can best speak for itself when it can *gather together* in some way to hear the arguments on the various sides of an issue and then, after face-to-face discussion, come to a collective decision. The image of the New England town meeting or the Athenian Assembly provides a picture of people discussing things democratically in one place. It is the long-standing model for how to conduct democracy under conditions where not only does everyone's vote count the same but social conditions have been provided that facilitate everyone's thinking through the issues together. We can call this image the *ideal of face-to-face democ-*

racy. A key issue in the continuing American experiment with democracy is: How can we adapt this ideal to the large-scale nation-state, to a population which cannot possibly gather together in the same room to take decisions?

Or can it? Some have thought that with modern technology, the country can, in a sense, gather together. Through technology we may be able to adapt the democracy of the town meeting to the large scale. But the gap between the town meeting proper and the "electronic town meeting" will prove nearly insurmountable.

What happens to the vote when the ideal of face-to-face democracy no longer applies? What happens when we vote without the social conditions that encourage everyone's gathering together in face-to-face discussion? Much of the continuing saga of the democratic idea can be thought of as an answer to that question. Voting in primaries or referendums, voting in general elections based on a "sound bite" of information or an impression culled from newspaper headlines, voting based on nothing more than name recognition or party label, or not voting at all (which has become the norm in the modern era)—these phenomena are quite different from voting in a small group after extensive face-to-face discussion. As we shall see, the American Founders struggled to adapt the ideal of face-to-face democracy to the large nation-state. But they thought it could be accomplished only through a system of *elected representation,* where the representatives would have the discussions and deliberations and come to decisions on behalf of the rest of us. Others, particularly the opponents of the Constitution who have come to be known as the anti-Federalists, wanted to place the locus of decision closer to the people, even if, for many issues, the ideal of face-to-face discussion could not be implemented. The beginnings of referendum democracy are built into the conflicts that arose at the founding.

The first major fork in the road came in Rhode Island, where opponents of the referendum concept argued that it could not fulfill the ideal of face-to-face democracy. Federalist supporters of the new Constitution argued that voting would not be meaningful unless everyone could gather together to hear the arguments on either side. The anti-Federalists agreed with the ideal but said that since it would be impossible to implement, they would go ahead and ask each citizen to vote. The anti-Federalists lost the battle over the Constitution (they were forced, after the referendum to hold a state convention that eventually approved it), but their picture of where American democracy would go has arguably triumphed in the long run, in the continuing process of democratic reform.

Magic Town was made in 1947, about a decade after George Gallup effectively launched the public opinion poll onto the national stage during the 1936 presidential election. From the beginning, Gallup offered the opinion poll as a serious instrument of democratic reform. But by the time of the Jimmy Stewart movie, very little of that notion was part of the public consciousness. The pollster was seen as someone who predicted elections in a competitive and cynical business. The Jimmy Stewart character prizes the discovery of Grandview as a shortcut to great profits. Only the citizens of Grandview understood the *responsibility* they bore: because people would think they spoke for the nation, they must be sure they had something worth saying.

After the "debacle" of Grandview's poll on a female president, the town became such a laughingstock that people began to leave. The city scrapped its plans for expansion. The remaining residents were demoralized and withdrew from public dialogue. They literally stopped speaking to one another. When asked survey questions, they all said they had "no opinion." They had ceased to be a "public." They had ceased to be effective citizens.

Faced with this demoralization and decline, the Jimmy Stewart and Jane Wyman characters try to revive the town with a scheme to go ahead with the suspended plans for the construction of a new high school. But it turns out that during the crisis, certain city leaders had conspired to sell the land. When confronted with the fact that city property could not be transferred without a vote, one of the town's leaders explains, "We intended to go through with the formality of a vote, but we just assumed that you people wouldn't care." The citizens are aroused by this response and decide to build the new school themselves, with the entire community donating its labor and expertise. The movie has a happy ending: this new example of civic cooperation saves the town's self-esteem, and it is lauded nationally in the media, which redeems the town's public image as well. The Jimmy Stewart and Jane Wyman characters are reconciled, and the movie ends amid scenes of hope and civic renewal.

This Hollywood ending is an instructive parable about community. How might it be possible in a society whose politics is dominated by opinion polls and elite manipulations to create the kind of civic engagement this microcosm of the country achieved by the end of the story? Is it possible to transform the entire country into "Magic Town," where citizens really care about the issues, where they are willing to think them through, and where they are also willing to contribute their time, resources, and labor to make their communities function? There is no easy answer to this question, but the continuing American process of experimentation makes it more of a possibility than our natural skepticism about Hollywood endings might support.

WHO SPEAKS FOR ME?

As a citizen, I have many "representatives." On a regular basis, I vote for a U.S. congressman, two U.S. senators, a governor, a lieutenant governor, a state senator, a state representative, six city council members (elected at large), a county commissioner for my district, the president and vice president of my school board (along with the school board member for my district), a mayor, nineteen county officials, and a number of other statewide office holders.

In addition, when I vote for the president of the United States my state elects thirty-two electors to the Electoral College. These people cast votes that represent me and the other residents of Texas in determining who should be the president. In the scheme of the American Founders, the electors were supposed to meet together, state by state, and deliberate on who was the most qualified candidate for president. As is true for many other representatives, their role has shrunk. Now, if they were to deliberate and depart from what the public had voted, they might well be condemned, or even prosecuted, as "faithless electors." Nevertheless, they represent me.

Here is a partial list of my elected representatives:

Federal Representatives
U.S. president: 1
U.S. vice president: 1
Presidential electors: 32
U.S. senators: 2
U.S. representative: 1
State Representatives
Governor of Texas: 1
Lieutenant governor of Texas: 1
Texas land commissioner: 1
Texas agriculture commissioner: 1
Texas comptroller: 1
Texas treasurer: 1
Texas attorney general: 1
Railroad commissioner: 3
State senator: 1
State representative: 1
Texas Supreme Court (including chief justice): 9
Texas Court of Criminal Appeals (including presiding judge): 9
Third Court of Appeals: 6
State district judge: 1
County Representatives
County judge: 1
County commissioner: 1 (per precinct)

County sheriff: 1
County tax assessor-collector: 1
County constable: 1 (per precinct)
District attorney: 1
Public weigher: 1
Judges, County Court at Law: 7
District clerk: 1
County clerk: 1
County treasurer: 1
County surveyor: 1
Justice of the peace: 1 (per precinct)
Municipal Representatives
Mayor of Austin: 1
City council members (at large): 6
School Board (Austin Independent School District)
President: 1
Vice president: 1
Member for my district: 1

There are also special districts for water control, the regional transit authority, and public utilities. These districts all have elected officials who represent me. It is instructive to discover that the various government officials I asked cannot even tell me how many elected officials represent me, primarily because no one seems to know how many of these special districts there may be. I have been advised that the only way to find out is to file "freedom of information" requests requiring the government to tell me. At the time of this writing, this process has not yet yielded a definitive list.

I find it revealing that an ordinary citizen can encounter such difficulty in simply attempting to determine the *number* of elected representatives he or she may have. Obviously, most citizens will not go to so much trouble, and they probably have no idea of how many people represent them, much less of the merits of the competing candidates for many of those elected positions.

But these federal, state, and local officeholders are only some of my elected representatives. Consider the political parties. There are 232 delegates who represent me at the Democratic National Convention if I choose to vote Democratic and 121 delegates to the Republican National Convention if I choose to vote Republican in the Texas primary in any given presidential election year. (Texas does not have party registration, and I may decide on the day of the primary which party I wish to vote in.) These delegates represent me in the nomination process of the president of the United States (assuming that I choose to vote in the primaries of one of the two major parties) just as the electors to the Electoral College represent me in the general election. If we add it all up, there are at least 200 and perhaps more than 350 people who purport to represent me.

I know almost nothing about most of these 200 to 350 people, and they certainly know almost nothing of me. Yet it is a common pretense of political discourse that we are supposed to have a *relationship:* these elected officials are "my" representatives. Consider what a citizen would have to learn even to come close to making an informed choice about these candidates, or to evaluating how well they have done their jobs. In many surveys over the past two decades, only about a quarter of American citizens could identify both of the senators from their state, and only slightly more could identify the name of their congressman. Yet these two are surely among the most prominent of the many offices a citizen may be asked to vote on. In a number of polls, little more than half the American citizens knew *which party* was in control of the U.S. Senate and less than a third knew that a member of Congress serves two-year terms. And while I do know that at the time of this writing Kay Bailey Hutchinson and Phil Gramm are my senators, most of us surely know virtually nothing about the Third Court of Appeals (or its equivalent in your state) or about the delegates who represent us at the national political conventions.

Many people, of course, pay little attention to the individual candidates and, instead, vote for a party. For several years, however, the proportion of American voters who identify themselves as Independents rather than as members of one party or another has gone up substantially. It is now greater than the number of identifiers with *either* of the two major parties. By 1992, 39 percent of voters categorized themselves as Independents, compared to 35 percent who called themselves Democrats and 26 percent, Republicans. And while many Independents will "lean" toward either the Democrats or the Republicans, the number of people who identify "strongly" with either party is also sharply in decline. Furthermore, enthusiasm for *either* party (as measured by "thermometer readings" in polls of support) has reached an all-time low, at least by the time of the 1994 elections.

Once voters leave the comparative simplicity of the two-party system, there is a dizzying variety of choices to be considered. Even if we stick to presidential elections, there have been 173 third parties since 1920 that have received at least a thousand votes. Of course, only five of these parties received even 5 percent of the votes. Many of them are tiny fringe groups with names like Take Back America or the Grassroots Party or the Down with Lawyers Party. Apart from the remarkable effort by Ross Perot, financed with expenditures of personal wealth comparable to the expenditures of the two major parties, the third parties in 1992 divided approximately 670,000 votes in an election in which more than 104 million votes were cast.[3] Excluding Perot, all the third-party candidates combined received about six-tenths of 1 percent of the vote.

But even if one thinks only of the candidates offered by the two major parties, the complexity of the choices offered is overwhelming. An ideal citizen might spend a great proportion of time reading campaign literature, questioning candidates in local forums or town meetings, and discussing the positions the competing candidates take on the issues with friends and colleagues. For good reasons, however, most of us are unlikely to become engaged in the process to the point where we could begin to discuss *all* the issues intelligently. Perhaps the occasional race for senator or governor will attract our interest, but such fits of attention will be the exception and not the rule for most of the choices we are regularly called on to make as citizens.

Once elected, the worlds these representatives inhabit are as distant from my world, the world of my everyday life, as is a parallel universe in a science-fiction story.[4] Like beings from a parallel universe, those on the other side of the divide can sometimes connect to my world via the magic of some technological innovation. In this case, the technologies that cross into my world, and make a kind of connection, tend to be television and radio. I get glimpses of these beings on television, and I hear their voices on radio talk shows. For the most part, however, their world does not seem to have much to do with mine. Their world does not connect to the world of my everyday life and my everyday welfare.

The only tangible, direct contact I get regularly from the world of my representatives is solicitation, by direct mail, for money. Would you give money to beings from a parallel universe whose images appeared in your living room? It is no wonder that by every measure of alienation, Americans feel distant, and expect little, from their elected representatives.

In using the metaphor of parallel universes, I do not wish to impugn the integrity or the motives of the many thousands of political actors who inhabit the special world of elective politics. I wish rather to emphasize how far we have come from the early hopes for representation—that it would "re-present" the people in a more thoughtful and enlightened form, "refining and enlarging the public views by passing them through a chosen body of citizens" to use James Madison's famous formulation in *Federalist* no. 10. Instead of a better version, a "refined" version, of our world, or an improved version of the people that is still recognizable as *us,* we now tend to see our representatives as alien—as inhabitants of a foreign territory.

At the same time, these representatives take on the appearance of clones, or synthetic re-creations of ordinary people. They use sophisticated techniques of polling and focus groups to find out what we want to hear, and then they tell us. A public image is synthesized, often by hired experts, and the presentation of that public image is carefully managed. We are conscious enough of the process by which these images are produced, however, that we often do not believe the speakers. We have become too conscious of the packaging to accept, unhesitatingly, the image it is meant to present.

Hence, despite their many efforts to keep in touch, my representatives still seem alien. They may have been ordinary persons once, but it is as if, in getting elected, they are subjected to a subtle process of transformation. From the standpoint of many citizens, these representatives have become automata who maintain a surface similarity to ordinary citizens in their statements and actions. Electing them might best be compared to the process by which alien copies replace ordinary people in *Invasion of the Body Snatchers.*

OUT OF THE CAVE?

The sense of unreality that applies to the official world of politics can be expressed in another way. Think back to the most celebrated image in political philosophy. Some 2,300 years ago, Plato offered a diagnosis of why the common people are not fit to rule. In his "allegory of the cave" he asked us to: "Imagine the condition of men living in a sort of cavernous chamber underground. Here they have been from childhood, chained by the leg and also by the neck, so that they cannot move and can see only what is in front of them, because the chains will not let them turn their heads."[5] They watch manipulated images, reflected from a fire onto the walls of the cave—a kind of puppet show, with images and voices. This is the only reality of which they are aware, so they think the images in the cave are the real world. They offer prizes to each other to see who can best predict the sequences of images with which they are presented. Such predictions count for insight or wisdom among the denizens of the cave.

In the modern age, our citizens live in a high-tech version of Plato's cave. Plato's allegory must seem less surprising to modern readers than it must have been to those of earlier periods because, like the inhabitants of Plato's cave, we receive our picture of the world, especially our picture of the political world, from reflected images and echoed voices. Instead of puppetlike reflections from fire on a cave wall, we watch television images in our living rooms. Instead of echoed voices from the puppet manipulators, we listen to the voices of radio and television talk shows and advertisements. Like the inhabitants of Plato's cave, we tend to take these reflected images and voices as the real world. At least in terms of our roles as citizens, things that do not happen on television have little, if any, force, vividness, or immediacy. It is the reflected images that seem real and important. They constitute the political world rather than what we can see outside "the cave" with our own eyes.

As I write this, the U.S. Army has troops in about seventy countries around the world. The U.N. has undertaken a major peace-keeping operation in Cambodia. There is a war raging in the Sudan. The U.S. military is feeding about 20,000 Kurds in northern Iraq. Because television has generally ignored these developments, the majority of the American public has virtually no awareness of them. In terms of the politics that counts, if something is not on television, it hasn't happened. Many television viewers, like the denizens of Plato's cave, who can look only at the reflected images, know little of any other world. By the time the current generation of children reaches the age of 18, its members, on average, will have logged 15,000 hours in front of a television set, more time than they will have spent in school.[6]

If we believe in democracy, can we somehow get citizens who are more prepared to exercise public responsibilities? Plato was no democrat, of course, and he offered the elitist solution of requiring many years of rigorous study to achieve the wisdom that might qualify a few for roles like that of the philosopher-king. But in his later work he treated this solution as utopian and offered, in the *Laws,* a role for samples of ordinary citizens chosen by lot who would make important public decisions in deliberative councils. He also developed a defense of what we would now call the separation of powers, a defense that influenced the Baron de Montesquieu and, via Montesquieu, the American Founders. Without a philosopher-king, Plato realized in his later work, power must be given to ordinary people, but under conditions where their good judgment can be encouraged and where a separation of powers can protect against tyranny and folly.[7]

This was, in essence, the complex problem faced more than two millennia later by the American Founders: how to give power to the people or their representatives so that "the deliberative sense of the community should govern," to use Hamilton's phrase, and so that the people could be protected from factions that might infringe upon the rights of others.[8] The American process of bold experimentation in grappling with this problem belongs not just to history books and revered, long-dead figures. It is a living process that occurs all around us, sometimes in subtle or unofficial ways, but one that continues, nevertheless.

If we accept the relevance of Plato's metaphor, the challenge remains: The people have a level of knowledge and wisdom comparable to the denizens of the cave. Yet if we believe in democracy (as Plato did not in the *Republic*) we need to somehow prepare the people to rule. Perhaps we can change the way information is presented to the cave dwellers, or perhaps we can engage people in real social problems, regardless of whether those problems appear on the evening news. Creating civic engagement at the local level and reforming the media to allow meaningful public input are two of the strategies for democratic reform I shall explore in this book. My subject will be the continuing transformations of democracy, both formal and informal, aimed at creating a society where citizens are thoughtful and engaged and their voice is worth listening to.

But what is the "voice of the people" if our citizens resemble the inhabitants of Plato's cave? The cave, very simply, becomes little more than an "echo chamber." Without any reference to Plato, the late V. O.

Key, Jr., put the situation aptly in a classic analysis: "The voice of the people is but an echo. The output of an echo chamber bears an inevitable and invariable relation to the input. As candidates and parties clamor for attention and vie for popular support, the people's verdict can be no more than a selective reflection from the alternatives and outlooks presented to them."[9]

Key's emphasis is on the onus the echo chamber places on elites, in politics and the media, to present the citizens in the echo chamber with information and positions that will permit them to evaluate alternatives responsibly. Like the inhabitants of the cave, the citizens in Key's chamber process only what is presented to them. Their opinions echo what they receive. The central problem of this book is whether the public voice can be *more* than an echo: Can the people take an active role in creating their voice and in determining what information they will need to deliberate and then speak? Although a positive answer requires changes both in the media and in the political process, there is, in fact, continuous experimentation in both areas, which produces ways for the people to achieve more than an echo.

2

WHO SPEAKS FOR THE PEOPLE?

NEW BEGINNINGS

American democracy continually re-creates itself in the name of one vision or another of the democratic idea. The founding of the country was a gamble against all conventional wisdom at the time, and the process of bold experimentation has continued ever since. Changing institutions so that, somehow, they better speak for the people has been a continuing American preoccupation, a distinctly American process. Ironically, democratic change has itself been a source of continuity in our political identity.

The American Founders believed that they were faced with a unique problem. As Hamilton put it in *Federalist* no. 1, "It seems to have been reserved to the people of this country . . . to decide the important question, whether societies of men are really capable or not of establishing good government *from reflection and choice,* or whether they are forever destined to depend for their political constitutions on accident and force" (emphasis added).[1] Self-conscious institutional reform, guided by deliberation, was the basis for the American founding and for the debate surrounding it. But reform is also a continuing process of experimentation. At both the national and local levels, innovations born of competing visions of democracy continuously change our system. Although democratic changes obviously occur throughout the world, the continuing reinvention of democracy has been a distinctively American preoccupation.

One of the challenges spurring innovation is the subject of a 2,500-year-old—and still unresolved—debate: *How can we achieve a democracy of engaged citizens, a democracy of face-to-face discussion, in states that contain many thousands or even many millions of people?* This problem has its origins in ancient Greece, but Americans have been grappling with it in diverse ways now for more than two hundred years.

There is a hill in Athens called the Pnyx that was the home of the ancient Athenian Assembly, the original and most influential image of direct democracy. At the height of Athenian democracy, the Pnyx could seat about 6,000 people. The total citizenry of ancient Athens, however, varied from about 60,000 adult males in the time of Pericles (fifth century B.C.) to about 30,000 in the time of Demosthenes (fourth century B.C.). As one commentator notes, "In some Greek eyes, Athens was actually too large to be a proper polis," too large, in other words, to be a functioning political community.[2] Various measures were, in fact, adopted to limit the size of the citizenry. Citizens were sent away to start émigré communities; citizenship of parents on both sides of the family was introduced as a more restrictive basis for determining who could be citizens.

Yet it is a mistake to think of ancient Athens entirely on the model of direct democracy. There was a host of representative institutions that engaged the energies of citizens outside the Assembly (where only a fraction of the citizenry could gather at one time). These institutions were directed at a second important issue, one we have already encountered: *When and how do the people speak?* If the citizens cannot all be gathered together, even in a small city-state like Athens, then when and how do they speak, or who speaks for them? On which of the many occasions and through which of the many voices that *presume* to speak for the people is there a voice worth listening to?

The Athenian innovations directed at this problem were based on selection by lot, or random selection. There were citizens' juries and legislative commissions of five hundred or more chosen by lot, and the Council (which set the agenda for the Assembly) was also randomly selected, as were the occupants of seven hundred or more other posts. Constant rotation of these public officials through random selection made Athens a far more participatory society than a focus on the Assembly would suggest.

It is ironic that at the time of the American Constitutional Convention, the American Founders were forced to struggle against the conventional wisdom that democracy was a system limited to city-states because only in city-states, it was thought, could everyone gather together. In the key ancient city-state, Athens, it was no more true that "everyone" could gather together than it was in the American states at the time of the Founders' deliberations. The ancient Athenians had to employ representation, although their version took a different form than that of the Founders.

Nevertheless, direct democracy in the Assembly did play a key role in Athenian politics. And in the ancient democracies, the number of men who could debate the issues collectively was limited, as Aristotle said, by the reach of a loud human voice, like that of the orator Stentor (who gave us the adjective *stentorian*).[3] It might be thought that in an age of electronic amplification and broadcasting such limits could be overcome. But technology is not, by itself, the solution. There is a sense in which television, for example, can now gather us together, but it is doubtful that it can do so in a way that lives up to all the democratic aspirations I shall explore here.[4]

Even the tiny eighteenth-century American states were of a size best ruled by monarchies, or so the political science of the time recommended. The Founders' limited picture of ancient democracies led them to draw the contrast between the ancient city-states and their own bold effort as marking the difference between direct and representative democracy—which they termed the distinction between a "democracy" (direct) and a "republic" (a representative structure). As

Madison explains in *Federalist* no. 14: "In a democracy the people meet and exercise the government in person; in a republic they assemble and administer it by their representatives and agents. A democracy consequently, must be confined to a small spot. A republic may be extended over a large region."

Yet if the Founders had had a more complete picture of Athenian democracy (or, for all the historical record can show, of any of the other ancient democracies),[5] they would have realized that even the ancient city-states were too large for a direct democracy, at least if it consisted principally of an assembly of citizens debating the issues when they were all gathered together.[6] Hence, the Athenians grappled in their own way with the same problem that was later to confront the American Founders. In different social contexts both groups dealt with the problem of scale—the problem posed by the number of citizens who had to be brought into a meaningful process of participation. And both relied on a form of representation to adapt a form of democratic rule to entities larger than could gather in one place. Although selection by lot differed from the answer chosen by the American Founders (direct and indirect elections), it served a similar purpose—it identified groups of manageable size who could gather, deliberate on the issues face to face, and speak for the entire citizenry.

In different ways, both the Athenians and the American Founders developed methods for fulfilling a simple and commonsense notion—*the ideal of face-to-face democracy*. It is an ideal so obvious that its relevance usually goes unstated. It is that the people, either directly or through their representatives, should meet together to hear competing arguments and discuss the issues in preparation for collective decisions. Voting, separated from a social context that makes this kind of face-to-face deliberation possible, becomes less meaningful. Without it voters are ill-prepared to make decisions. They have not heard the competing arguments, they have not had a chance to raise objections and counterarguments. They may even have little reason to pay attention. An intelligent basis for decision making requires a social context that effectively motivates people to pay attention and to deliberate on the issues. The problem is that this social context, easily realized in a small group, is difficult to achieve in a large nation-state.

The Athenians realized an extraordinarily high level of participation and mass citizen engagement with the issues, at least among those whom they designated citizens. Such levels have never been matched, in a sustained way, by any large modern nation-state. Indeed, the American Founders never expected—and even feared—mass participation. *Their* democracy was an elite republic of elected representatives who would deliberate together and speak *for* the people. The Founders could realize the ideal of face-to-face democracy for the people's elected representatives, even if they could not achieve it for the people themselves.

Yet the vision of a democracy that could somehow fulfill this ideal for all the people and not merely for their representatives—a democracy with sustained mass participation and citizen engagement with public issues—came to guide changes in American democracy and, to a considerable degree, changes in democracies throughout the world. The problem is that adapting that vision to the large (even gigantic) scale of the modern nation-state remains an unsettled—and only partially solved—problem. Often reformers aspiring to the ideal have instead achieved a democracy of atomized, individual voters who have no effective motivation to think through the issues or discuss them with other citizens.

Why should this vision be so difficult to achieve? One of the most important impediments was identified by the economist Anthony Downs in a classic work in 1956.[7] Citizens in large nation-states have incentives to be "rationally ignorant." If I have only one vote in millions, why should I spend a lot of time and effort attempting to inform myself about the positions of competing candidates, competing parties, or competing alternatives in an election or a referendum? My individual vote has such a small chance of making any difference to the outcome that time and effort invested in deciding how best to cast that vote will not make any appreciable difference. Of course, if I am interested in politics for its entertainment value (perhaps because I have peculiar preferences) or if I have some special role that affords me more influence than most people have on the outcome, it might well be worthwhile to spend the time and effort needed to think about the issues or the differences between candidates or parties. But for most citizens, ignorance is, unfortunately, the rational choice, in the sense that the time and effort required to overcome it do not represent a reasonable investment. Individually or collectively, we can have more impact, if we desire it, in other ways.

This argument does not depend on my motivations' being selfish, or on my political agenda's being connected to my personal interests. The argument is fundamentally the same even if my motives are entirely altruistic. If I wish, for example, to help the homeless or save the environment, making special efforts to acquire political information about the candidates' stands on these issues is as irrational a method of pursuing those agendas—at least so far as information would better guide my individual voting decision—as it would be for a purely self-interested agenda. Because the individual voting decision has only a minuscule probability of making any difference to the outcome, efforts to better direct that decision will not make any appreciable difference either. The same problem of collective action confronts the altruistic and the self-interested alike.

Of course, I may acquire a fair amount of political information in the course of my day-to-day living. I may learn, for example, about the economy and interest rates because I want to buy a house or a car. My friends may be unemployed, or I may find out about dramatic disasters through the media. Some political scientists have argued that *as a by-product* of the other activities we rationally pursue, we acquire a certain amount of political information in any case. With this information, I can react to certain "cues" given by candidates about where they stand and come to conclusions about how to vote (if, indeed, I can be motivated to vote).[8] While there is certainly some truth to this observation, we shall see that it falls far short of the levels of engagement with the issues required by the democratic aspirations discussed here.

The movement toward more direct democracy, often actuated by a vision of something not unlike the Athenian Assembly or the New England town meeting, in fact results in the decision-making power, in the large nation-state, being brought to a people who are *not a public*. The locus of ostensible decision resides in millions of disconnected and inattentive citizens, who may react to vague impressions of headlines or shrinking sound bites but who have no rational motivation to pay attention so as to achieve a collective engagement with public problems. In a host of formal and informal changes, we have brought power to the people: there are now primaries and referendums rather than decisions by elites in smoke-filled rooms, direct rather than indirect election of senators, and an almost daily stream of opinion polls telling us what "we think"—when most of us are barely paying attention. While there is a limited sense in which these changes bring "power to the people" they do so under conditions that often approach collective sedation on how the people are to exercise their power.

Of course, the mass public is not always disengaged. Sometimes specific groups are aroused. The mere fact of intensity of feeling, however, should not overcome our worries about information and shared deliberation on the issues. Consider a second ancient model of democracy, very different from the extended debate in the Athenian Assembly or in its citizens' juries or randomly selected legislative commissions.

In ancient Sparta, members of the Council were elected by a method called the Shout.[9] The order in which candidates to the Council were considered was determined by lot. This order was not known to the impartial evaluators who were seated in another room with writing tablets. The evaluators' job was simply to assess the loudness of the cheering each candidate received when he walked in front of the assembled throng. The candidate receiving the loudest shouts and applause was deemed the winner. Missing in the Spartan method was the entire social context of careful debate and deliberative argument fostered by the Athenian institutions of the Assembly, the citizens' juries, the legislative commissions, and the Council. Aristotle dismissed the Spartan applaudometer as childish. Yet if we ask which model of ancient democracy we have come closer to realizing in our modern quest for direct democracy, we must concede that there are ways in which the Spartan model is closer than the Athenian to contemporary practices.

Consider the spectacle that unfolded when President Clinton's nominee for attorney general, Zoë Baird, was identified as having hired a couple of illegal aliens as domestic help (and as having failed to pay their Social Security taxes). The public outcry from nearly half a million people phoning Congress in a single day sank the nomination. It is undoubtedly the case that most of the callers did not follow the nuances of Baird's complex confirmation hearing. Rather, radio talk-show hosts stimulated a negative "shout" based on an offensive sound bite. The intensity of the public reaction was judged from faxes and phone calls and tabulated by staff in Congress and the White House. Later in Clinton's term, the White House was organized to tabulate reactions coming from about 65,000 calls a day when the president's economic plan was under consideration.

As Michael Wines summarizes the new electronic wiring between citizens and government, Washington's "principal problem is not that it listens too little, but that it listens—and is shouted at—too much." As he explains, with only a little hyperbole: "Modern Washington is wired for quadraphonic sound and wide-screen video, lashed by fax, computer, 800 number, overnight poll, FedEx, grassroots mail, air shuttle and CNN to every citizen in every village on the continent and Hawaii too." Moreover, the connection is two-way. "Its every twitch is blared to the world, thanks to C-Span, open-meeting laws, financial disclosure reports and campaign spending rules, and its every misstep is logged in a database for the use of some future office-seeker."[10]

Obviously, technology has been harnessed in service to a kind of democracy, one which gives the large nation-state a system that is reminiscent of ancient Greece. But to the extent that the numbers and intensity of the decision makers are being tabulated independent of a social context that permits real collective deliberation on complex issues, it is the Spartan rather than the Athenian ideal of ancient democracy that is being realized. The sting of an offensive sound bite arouses a populace that is only sound-bitten. The ire of talk-show democracy has given us a mass electronic version of the Shout.

The basic diagnosis for our arrival at this impasse is that the ideal of face-to-face democracy does not translate directly to the large nation-state. When a decision is placed in the hands of millions of people rather than a small group who can gather in a single room, the social conditions that might motivate discussion and deliberation are largely suppressed, because of the incentives created for rational ignorance. Nobody intended it to be so. But the unintended consequence of many well-meaning democratic reforms and related informal changes is that we have lost the social conditions that would reasonably motivate collective discussion by an informed public over a sustained period. Efforts are being made at both the national and local levels to re-create those conditions, and such efforts are an important part of the American process of renewal and experimentation. Several will be discussed here. Nevertheless, the basic story is that in democratizing our system we have, paradoxically, tended to empty that system of seriously engaged citizens.[11]

Democracy by public opinion changes the incentives not only for voters to pay attention but also for leaders to do anything other than what voters tell them. The problem has been apparent for a long time and has only been exacerbated by the increased use of technology and opinion polling to keep "leaders" in touch with voters. As Winston Churchill said, in a speech to the House of Commons in 1941, "I see that a speaker at the week-end said that this was a time when leaders should keep their ears to the ground. All I can say is that the British nation will find it very hard to look up to leaders who are detected in that somewhat ungainly posture."[12] Churchill always exercised a leadership people could look up to—but by not keeping his ear to the ground he found himself unexpectedly out of office at the height of his triumph in World War II.

A VOICE FROM RHODE ISLAND

The battle lines over the ideal of face-to-face democracy were drawn in a long-forgotten skirmish in the creation of the American Republic—the referendum conducted by the people of Rhode Island over ratification of the U.S. Constitution. This referendum marks a fork in the road for American democracy. Down one road, we would have kept the conditions that make deliberation together possible, even if we would thereby have limited participation. Traveling the other road, we emphasize participation even when conditions for deliberation and discussion are absent. The first road was defended by the Founders; the second road leads to referendums, primaries, and the other institutions of mass democracy.

The Rhode Island debate over the appropriateness of a referendum returns us to one of our basic questions: When and how do the people speak? If democracy is to be a system guided, to some degree, by the voice of the people, which voice or voices are authoritative? Which voices speak for the citizenry of any given state or of the entire country?

At first glance, it might seem as if there is no great mystery about this question. In a modern context, one answer seems increasingly obvious: the people *speak for themselves*. All we need do is *ask* them, in aggregate, by holding a referendum. Or, if asking everyone is too much trouble for the occasion in question, we ask a representative sample by conducting an opinion poll.

In 1788 Rhode Island's Assembly, when asked to ratify the proposed U.S. Constitution, came up with precisely that answer. Instead of the elected "state convention" of representatives (the mode of approval for the Constitution specified at Philadelphia), the Assembly decided to take the issue directly to the people. It was argued that since "the People were called upon to surrender a Part of their Liberties that They were the best judges what Part they ought to give up."

This proposal was held by critics to be completely novel: "This Mode was without Precedent on the Face of the Earth," they charged. Yet it was actually preceded by earlier practices in Rhode Island itself, as well as in other New England states. The Rhode Island Constitution of 1641 had asserted that Rhode Island was to have a "Democratical or Popular Government. . . . It is in the Power of the Body of Freemen, orderly assembled, or the major part of them, to make or constitute Just Lawes." And Massachusetts had previously rejected its state constitution in a vote taken at town meetings throughout the state in 1778.

Note the requirement that decisions in Rhode Island be made "by the Body of Freemen, *orderly assembled*" and note that the Massachusetts vote, like the one in Rhode Island, was held in town meetings throughout the state, where at least the local people could debate the issues before taking a vote. Our modern notion of a referendum consisting of isolated voters who cast their votes at polling places without any apparatus of collective gathering for discussion had not yet developed. But it had its germ in these early movements toward *direct* consultation with the people.

Even earlier methods of direct democracy in Swiss cantons provided another kind of precedent. Swiss practices for directly consulting the people were clearly closer to our ideal of gathering everyone together—precisely the ideal Federalist critics of the referendum were to argue would have to be sacrificed by the new device. In many of the Swiss cantons, there had long been *Landsgemeinden,* annual gatherings that every adult male citizen was required to attend, where the people directly considered proposed legislation. An important difference between this and the Federalist model is that the *entire* adult male citizenry was required to gather in a single place to debate the issues. The Swiss had managed to maintain conditions, at least at the local level, that allowed something similar to the ideal of face-to-face

27

democracy to be realized. The American Federalists, who boycotted the Rhode Island referendum, would have had no argument with the desirability of the Swiss method. But they declared such a gathering impossible even for a state the size of Rhode Island (population about 69,000 at that time).

The Federalists' position was that a serious consideration of the issues, where argument could be met by counterargument, required citizens to *meet together* in preparation for a vote. Because it would be impossible for the entire citizenry to meet together, consideration by a representative body was the only way the proposed new Constitution could receive a thoughtful hearing. "As it is inconvenient, and perhaps even impossible, in a State no larger than this for all the individuals to assemble together, it was therefore necessary from the nature of things to introduce the idea of representation." With representatives of all parts of the state, "all the interests, trades and professions" could be part of the same discussion. "Having the collected sense and wisdom of a free people," the representatives "could reason, confer and convince each other." To ask the citizens to judge separately, in towns scattered throughout the state, would be to ask them to decide with partial knowledge, partial arguments, and unanswered misrepresentations. Such a decision, the Federalists argued, "could not be considered as decisive" because it would not have been taken "from *the people in their assembled collective capacity,* the only mode in which a major vote is considered to be binding on the minority."[13] It is precisely this assembled collective capacity that fulfills what I have been calling the ideal of face-to-face democracy.

Similar arguments were made by the Freemen of Providence, who objected to the planned referendum, in a town meeting a month later. They specifically endorsed our ideal, which they called "the most natural and simple idea of the mode of proceeding":

> All the people should be assembled on some spacious plain, to consult on the subject, discuss and adopt a constitution for them-

selves. In ancient times, and in small republics, this measure has been taken with success, but in the present case, where is the spot commodious for assembling all the freemen of this State?—And where is the man who could be heard to advantage by such a numerous assembly.[14]

Because of such considerations, therefore, "the doctrine of Representation will force itself on our minds in an instant." The Freemen of Providence agreed with the Federalists and recommended a state convention "to have their reasons discussed with candour and deliberation"—a goal they felt could not be accomplished in separate town meetings representing purely local interests, where the arguments would differ from one meeting to the next.

The move for a state convention failed, however; the proposed referendum was boycotted by the Federalists; and the anti-Federalists carried the vote against the Constitution. Only after all the other states had approved the Constitution by the prescribed method of state conventions (North Carolina needed two tries),[15] and only after the new U.S. Senate passed a bill that would impose a further boycott on Rhode Island, cutting it off from shipping with the other states, and only after plans were publicly discussed for invading Rhode Island and splitting the land between Massachusetts and Connecticut was the new Constitution finally ratified in a state convention on May 29, 1790. Only, that is, by returning to the ideal of gathering everyone together through a state convention—admittedly, under the threat of isolation, and even possible dismemberment[16]—did Rhode Island finally ratify the Constitution.

It is worth observing that the debate in Rhode Island over how to enable everyone to discuss the issues together in preparation for a decision was a debate built into the colony's foundations. Its early history embodied the ideal of face-to-face democracy in its original political organization. According to one of the first definitive histories, "The government established by these primitive settlers of Providence was an anomaly in the history of the world. At the outset it was a pure democracy. . . . As yet there was no delegated power."[17] As the colony grew, elements of representative government were introduced, until by 1647 a system combining individual discussion with representation was finally adopted. According to this system, "all laws were to be first discussed in the towns. The town first proposing it was to agitate the question in town meeting and conclude by vote." If a proposal passed in a particular town it was sent to other towns. A proposal passing all four towns was sent "to a committee of six men from each town, freely chosen. . . . If they found the majority of the colony concurred, . . . it was to stand as a law 'till the next General Assembly of all the people,' who were finally to decide whether it should continue as law or not."[18]

Although this system introduced elements of representative government, it was a remarkable attempt to accommodate something that approached the ideal of face-to-face democracy on a continuing basis, even though the population of the colony was growing to a point where this ideal would become impossible (as it clearly was, more than a century and a quarter later, at the time of the referendum debate).

WHAT SHOULD REPRESENTATIVES DO?

The debate on the Rhode Island referendum turned on the primacy of face-to-face democracy. The Federalists argued that the way to make a decision was to gather everyone in the same room, let them hear all the arguments on either side, and then take a decision. Because it was impossible for all the citizens of the state to gather in one place, the Federalists argued that a convention of elected officials would permit the same ideal to be realized for a body of representatives, who would make an informed decision in the name of the people. The anti-Federalists, by contrast, chose to take the issue directly to the people, regardless of whether those voting would have a chance to hear all the arguments and thus make an informed decision.

But even in cases where the people chose representatives, there was another, similar debate going on, both in America and in Britain, about whether those representatives should receive "instructions" from the people. If elected representatives are bound to obey instructions from their constituents, then it will not matter whether they gather in one room to hear all the arguments. Their votes will already have been determined by constituents at home, who will not have had the benefit of those deliberations.

The most famous proponent of the elite deliberations of an elected parliament, Edmund Burke, experienced the conflict between his constituent's views and the independent judgments he wished to defend. In a famous speech to the Electors of Bristol on the occasion of his being chosen to represent them in Parliament in November 1774, he explained that members of Parliament had to maintain their independence in order to deliberate together.

Burke, in agreeing to stand for the seat at Bristol, came directly into the controversy about whether representatives should be "instructed." The preceding member had faced demands that he accept instruction. Burke's running partner in that very election agreed to accept instructions. But Burke argued, in what became a famous defense of the independence of elected representatives, that members of Parliament needed to be free to decide conscientiously what was in the best interests of their constituents after they had had the opportunity to hear and discuss the arguments together. "Government and legislation are matters of reason and judgement" he argued, not matters merely of "will." To abide by instructions would produce an absurd situation: "What sort of reason is that in which the determination precedes the discussion; in which one set of men deliberate and another decide; and where those who perform the conclusion are perhaps three hundred miles distant from those who hear the arguments?" The voters at home could not hear the arguments and counterarguments. To demand that their views be followed by those who could would be to make "a fundamental mistake."[19]

Burke elaborated his argument by distinguishing between a *congress* and a *parliament.* By *congress,* he meant a gathering of ambassadors, as in an international treaty negotiation. Representing their countries, ambassadors are naturally bound by instructions from their respective states. But a *parliament,* in Burke's view, was not like that. It was more properly a deliberative assembly, in which face-to-face discussions would permit the representatives to exercise informed judgment. Ironically, Burke's term for the nondeliberative assembly, a congress bound by instructions, became the term for America's representative institution. Congressional representation offers us a history of attempts to fend off formal instructions by state legislatures (which originally selected senators) and informal instructions by constituents. In spite of two centuries of attempts to defend elite deliberation, it is arguable that the Congress we have finally developed is close enough to being an instructed body, at least on many issues, that there is no longer any irony in the choice of terms.

In any case, Burke's argument was that a parliament was a deliberative assembly and not a congress:

> Parliament is not a *congress* of ambassadors from different and hostile interests; which interests each must maintain, as an agent and advocate, against other agents and advocates, but parliament is a *deliberative* assembly of *one* nation, with *one* interest, that of the whole; where, not local purposes, not local prejudices, ought to guide, but the general good, resulting from the general reason of the whole. You choose a member indeed; but when you have chosen him, he is not member of Bristol, but he is a member of *parliament.*[20]

Burke found that in exercising his independent judgment, regardless of the views of his constituents, he alienated them, both on the American question and by his support for Catholic and Irish emancipation. He was voted out for departing from the views of his constituents; and he managed to maintain a position in Parliament solely because Lord Rockingham gave him a seat from a "rotten borough" (one with a small number of constituents, under the control of a wealthy patron). Burke's bold words, which best articulate the role of an independent legislator, defined a role that was too independent for his own constituents. Only a seat beyond the control of the people kept his influential voice in the "deliberative assembly."

Burke was undoubtedly acting from his political convictions and his sense of the long-term interests of the country. He was rewarded as many legislators who have followed his advice have been rewarded since. Consider this recent example, cited by *Roll Call,* a journal that covers Congress, in a 1993 editorial: "Last year, one courageous House Member took to the floor to say: 'You do not have to accept public opinion. You can change it. You can form it. You can shape it. You can enlighten it. . . . If this House is willing in a moment of political passion to set aside the very thing that we are sworn to uphold, then public opinion be damned.'" As the editorial noted, Rep. Dave Nagle (D., Iowa) was defeated in the next election.[21] And in our democratic system, there were no patrons who controlled another seat for him to go to, as in Burke's case. Modern democracy, in its responsiveness to public opinion, expects public servants to act as such. This responsiveness helps fulfill a worthy vision of democracy. But it often exacts a heavy price in deliberation, by tying representatives to the vagaries of public opinion.

THE MOST NATURAL AND SIMPLE IDEA

Face-to-face democracy singles out an implicit and only partially stated ideal. Its progressive abandonment, as the numbers of people to be consulted have grown, will be a continuing topic of this book. In the meantime, let us pause to consider the conditions under which this "most natural and simple idea" yields a defensible version of democracy.

Envision a small group democracy: Everyone is gathered together.

After a full discussion, where the issues are debated in depth and the conflicting sides have a full hearing, a decision is taken in which each person's vote counts equally. This is our common picture of an engaged democracy. There is, of course, no guarantee that the group's decisions will be wise or even right. Groups as well as individuals can make terrible mistakes. But there is no doubt that *if* democracy is defensible, it is most defensible in this kind of small group context.

For under the conditions just described, a collective process occurs in which the group has a reasonable chance to form its collective, considered judgments—to give its public voice, if you will, to the topic in question. Arguments on rival positions get an extended hearing, and each side has a chance to answer the other. The same information is available to all. People are present and engaged by the process. They do not merely listen. They also participate, in a context which is small enough that each can credibly believe that his or her individual voice counts. And they discuss the issues in an atmosphere of mutual respect, attempting to find common ground. The point of the deliberations is not to deprive some of their rights but rather to find a solution all can live with. And finally, when votes are taken, the preferences of all participants are counted in the same way.

These factors can be broken down into four simple conditions:

Political Equality: citizens' preferences count equally in a process that can plausibly be viewed as representative of everyone.

Deliberation: a wide range of competing arguments is given careful consideration in small-group, face-to-face discussion.

Participation: a significant proportion of the citizenry is engaged in the process.

Non-tyranny: the political process avoids, whenever possible, depriving any portion of the citizenry of rights or essential interests. Even when the process is democratic in all the other senses just defined, it must also avoid the "tyranny of the majority."

COUNTING PEOPLE EQUALLY

Each of these conditions deserves discussion. What does it mean to say that citizens' preferences count equally? Obviously, if I have extra votes, my preferences count more than yours. John Stuart Mill advocated "plural voting"—giving more say to those with more competence and education—but the idea was never well received in democratic circles. Although it was the case in England until shortly after World War II that graduates of Oxford and Cambridge had an extra vote (because they could vote for an extra member of Parliament), the elimination of this peculiar arrangement was generally accepted as a useful democratic reform. Of course, the United States has its own peculiarities. A citizen of Rhode Island or Montana has many times the voting power of a citizen of California—insofar as elections to the U.S. Senate are concerned. The situation is no different, in principle, from the one Madison considered scandalous in Britain, where there were rotten boroughs. In *Federalist* no. 56, which was, after all, part of an extensive argument in favor of the proposed U.S. Constitution, Madison pointed out that out of 8 million inhabitants in Britain at the time, a total of 364 persons elected one-ninth of all the members of Parliament, and a total of 5,723 persons elected fully one-half of all the M.P.s. Madison's aim in this issue was to defend the House of Representatives proposed for the United States. To do so, he simply ignored the similar disparities in the number of citizens corresponding to each legislator that were built into the proposed Senate. Of course, at the time he was writing, the Senate was indirectly elected. Senators were selected by the state legislatures, so perhaps the differing number of citizens per senator did not appear as glaring an issue.

This contrast was not, of course, lost on critics of the proposed Constitution. "Brutus," a prominent anti-Federalist, asked: "How unreasonable, and unjust then is it, that Delaware should have a representation in the Senate, equal to Massachusetts, or Virginia? The latter of which contains ten times her numbers, and is to contribute to the aid of the general government in that proportion."[22]

Setting aside the historical anomaly of the U.S. Senate, the idea of political equality has a deep resonance in the American process of democratic reform. A proposal such as Mill's, for extra votes for the more intelligent or more educated, would be regarded as simply bizarre in any serious American context.

Yet counting votes equally is only part of any defensible account of political equality. Suppose, as is normally the case, that the number of people participating is less—sometimes a good deal less—than the total citizenry. In the presidential selection process, for example, all votes cast are counted equally, but the *order* among states effectively gives voters in some states a great deal more influence over the process than voters in other states. Furthermore, the electorates that actually participate are small and often unrepresentative of their respective states or of the nation as a whole. Because the "momentum" born in early primaries and caucuses, such as those in Iowa and New Hampshire, often determines whether candidates will even be viable when they reach states later in the process, there are serious questions of political equality to be raised about the process itself. Are those who make the effective decision representative of the electorate of the nation or even of the members of any given political party? Self-selected electorates in the early states end up, effectively, speaking for the nation regardless of how well they represent the rest of us.

The problem is even worse during the primary before the primaries, sometimes called the "invisible primary"—the period before the official events when candidates garner credibility for fundraising, for their standing with the media, and for building their campaign organizations. Bill Clinton in 1991 (and Jimmy Carter in 1975) dominated the invisible primary by winning a nonevent known as the Florida Straw Poll. By taking this occasion to garner support from party activists in one state he jumped ahead of the competition. His fundraising efforts took off after the December 1991 victory, and by releasing news of his lead in fundraising to the press, he was able to go into the official primary events with a great deal of press attention, for he was now the apparent front runner. The Florida Straw Poll did not even involve the mass of Democratic voters in the state. However, other candidates made the mistake of not taking the straw poll seriously. But both Bill Clinton and the media took it seriously enough that it became, as it had for Carter in 1976, an important vehicle for launching an effective candidacy by a man who was, otherwise, not well known.

Momentum in the primary season is born through media coverage of the early days of the contest. Hence, when "New Hampshire's primary received 125 times as much coverage per democratic voter as the large Ohio primary" (which occurred much later in the process), there is a sense in which political equality has been undermined.[23] New Hampshire voters, because of their position in the process, have so much more influence on the nomination than do Ohio voters that it is as if they had extra votes. Indeed, maps of the United States have been redrawn to illustrate New Hampshire in terms of its weight in the process—and they are unrecognizable to students of conventional geography.[24]

Arguably, if New Hampshire were a microcosm of the entire nation—if New Hampshire voters had, for example, the same mix of racial, ethnic, class, urban, and rural characteristics as the rest of the country—then such a process might offer a form of *representation* to voters later in the queue. New Hampshire might claim, like Magic Town, that its residents can, in a sense, speak for the nation. But given the demographic peculiarities of New Hampshire, such a notion is laughable. The thought, however, suggests an additional clause in how we need to formulate our criterion of political equality.

We can specify that political equality is served when those who participate are statistically representative of the entire citizenry and when the process of collective decision weighs their votes equally. Of course, if everyone participates, there is no problem about the group being statistically representative. But when there is a subgroup, and it differs substantially from the rest of the population, there is a sense in which those left out cannot view themselves as being represented. This is important because ultimately we are interested in the question: When and how do the people speak? And if the group purporting to speak for the people differs greatly from the people on whose behalf they "speak," then that lack of representativeness raises a serious question about whether the concerns and interests of those left out are being voiced.

One source of new voices purporting to speak for the people, for example, is talk-show democracy. But "electronic town meetings" rely on participants who are haphazardly collected, often based on self-selection by people with hidden agendas, or they conduct viewer call-in polls that overrepresent people who feel strongly about some issue of the moment; these gatherings routinely violate our criterion of political equality. Viewers or listeners who call in consist disproportionately of those who are angry or concerned about a particular issue. Treating the responses as the voice of all the people results in a real distortion. A 1993 study by the Times Mirror Center for the Press and the People found a strong right-wing and antigovernment tilt to talk-radio audiences in general, and to those who call in, in particular. Talk-radio callers speak for some of the people. The shows provide a useful forum for the airing of issues. But such shows cannot be taken as representations of what "the people think" without a scientific basis for such a conclusion in any particular case. As the study cautioned: "American public opinion is being distorted and exaggerated by the voices that dominate the airwaves of talk radio."

Viewer call-in polls are used for everything from pronouncing on the guilt or innocence of O. J. Simpson in a murder trial, to determining whether or not we should invade Haiti. Presenting self-selected polls as if they are the voice of the people is a misrepresentation—it simply introduces a pseudo-voice into the dialogue that purports to speak for us all.

Similar problems arise with pseudo-events based on self-selected participation. When the Iowa Republican Party conducts a straw poll of presidential preferences nineteen months before the Iowa caucuses, for example—open to anyone willing to buy a steak dinner—and then tabulates the results as an early indication of voter opinion, it is simply creating an occasion for unrepresentative distortion. There are problems even with scientific polls early in the presidential race. Many citizens will not yet have paid enough attention to the identities of candidates or their positions to have established well-formed preferences. Early poll results are likely to measure nothing more than name recognition. But when there is no scientific sample and when the participants select themselves, we make a fundamental error in thinking that they speak for anyone other than themselves.

When self-selected polls receive extensive coverage in the media, they have additional political effects. In 1980, ABC television tabulated the viewers calling in their instant reactions to a presidential debate between Jimmy Carter and Ronald Reagan. The viewers were asked to call a 900-number, which requires a charge, and which further distorted the composition of the public willing to call. The network used the resulting numbers to declare Reagan an instant two-to-one winner—a judgment that offered a sharply different picture of the contest from the one reached by random samples of the public (which initially scored the debate about even). Such distorted pictures of the public, when broadcast during the period people are crystallizing their impressions of the outcome, will, in turn, have an effect. A pseudo-representation of the people is, in effect, spin-doctoring the debate for the rest of us.

The same kind of thing happens on a smaller scale nearly every day in electronic town meetings with self-selected or haphazardly selected studio audiences. For example, the daily town meeting "Talk-Back Live," a one-hour show on CNN that confronts a current issue, often culminating in a vote by the studio audience. Although we are never told how the audience is selected, the implication is always that the vote is somehow a representation of public opinion—how the public in general would come to judge the issue in question were they too on the show. Such votes can be expected to influence public opinion among viewers just as the viewer call-in poll of the debate did. When apparent representations of the people violate political equality, then the voice of the people is distorted. But political equality, by itself, is not enough to guarantee that a representation of the people's voice is worth listening to.

DELIBERATION: THINKING THROUGH THE ISSUES TOGETHER

Instant reactions in a studio audience or in a viewer call-in also raise questions that speak to our second democratic condition—deliberation. To what degree do citizens have an opportunity to hear the full range of competing arguments that are regarded as crucial by participants in an ongoing public debate? To what degree are those citizens motivated to ponder and debate the issues? As a point of comparison, consider the purely imaginary ideal that the philosopher Jürgen Habermas calls the ideal speech situation. In this situation, all arguments are answered in a context of free and equal discussion. All arguments deemed relevant by anyone in the discussion are given as extensive a hearing as anyone wants and people are willing to consider all the arguments offered on their merits. We can imagine questions receiving a virtually unlimited amount of time so that, in the end, the only force leading to a resolution of any question is the "force of the better argument."[25]

The ideal speech situation defines a purely hypothetical—indeed, an impossible—benchmark, in which people make their decisions on the merits without any regard for what economists call decision costs: the time and effort required to reach an agreement. In the real world, people cannot ignore decision costs. Indeed, calculations about the decision costs for voters, given the paltry benefits and voters' lack of influence on the process, provide the basis for the conclusions about "rational ignorance" discussed earlier.

We can put the ideal speech situation at one extreme of an imaginary continuum and then imagine various forms of *incompleteness*—compared to this ideal—as we think about more realistic forms of deliberation. When arguments offered by some participants go unanswered by others, when information that would be required to understand the force of a claim is absent, or when some citizens are unwilling or unable to weigh some of the arguments in the debate, then the process is *less deliberative* because it is incomplete in the manner specified. In practical contexts a great deal of incompleteness must be tolerated. Hence, when we talk of improving deliberation, it is a matter of *improving* the completeness of the debate and the public's engagement with it, not a matter of perfecting it because that would be virtually impossible under realistic conditions. No plausible democratic reform can bring us to the ideal speech situation, but there are many changes that might take us a little closer than we are.

In addition to whether arguments are answered by counterarguments, we must also ask *who* is supposed to be doing the deliberating. The Congress, for example, may engage in a detailed discussion of some piece of legislation (although there is a great deal of room for improving deliberation in Congress as well),[26] but the public may receive no more than a sound bite or an impression drawn from headlines. On many issues, the elites may deliberate to a high degree and the public hardly at all, even though everyone is vaguely aware of the same issue at the same time. At bottom, a major part of the problem of democratic reform is how to promote *mass deliberation*—how to bring the people into the process under conditions where they can be engaged to think seriously and fully about public issues.

As we shall see, there are conditions that can sometimes make mass deliberation possible. When it does occur, it is different in character from a great deal of elite deliberation. When members of Congress consider an issue, they are naturally concerned with reelection, with publicity, and with the effect of their deliberations on public perceptions and on key interest groups and supporters—in addition to the merits of the issue. For ordinary people, the role of citizen does not carry with it the same institutional incentives. Ordinary citizens do not arrive at positions after consulting focus groups, polls, lobbyists, campaign consultants, and spin doctors. Ordinary citizens are not running for reelection.

Once again the rational ignorance that motivates an inattentive public means that much of what passes for public discourse must be reduced to a television sound bite. Studies of the 1988 presidential campaign produced a sensation by showing that the average sound bite on the network evening news had declined in length from about 42 seconds to about 9 seconds from 1968 to 1988. In the 1992 presidential campaign, the decline continued, to about 7.5 seconds.

A sound bite, for these purposes, is the period during which a presidential candidate speaks uninterrupted on the network evening news. The decline in the length of the sound bite reduced the effective political discourse reaching much of the public to messages worthy of fortune cookies or bumper stickers. Of course, there were other messages in other forums, such as talk shows, that permitted longer discussion. But it is the sound bite on the evening news that is typically the most widely disseminated and that actually penetrates the public consciousness. Indeed, many talk shows, like many televised debates in the primary season, are treated by candidates as occasions for the creation of new sound bites which then recycle around the system.

The brevity of the effective sound bite creates a limitation on the ability of public discourse to produce serious deliberation. Nine seconds (or seven and a half) is never enough time to say anything adequate to the complexity of important public problems. Hence when President Bush announces "Read my lips, no new taxes," or when President Clinton holds up a pen and promises to veto any health plan lacking universal coverage, the simplifications required to get the attention of the public—within the space of a single sound bite—filter out the information needed for deliberation about complex alternatives.

Citizens are rarely engaged enough by an issue to confront the trade-offs, the ways in which demanding more of one valued dimension may require making sacrifices along another. In 1994, as the national debate on health-care reform reached a crescendo, polls showed widespread support for a variety of conflicting goals. As Robert Blendon summed up public attitudes in one study, "One, lower my premiums, two, cover the uninsured, and lastly, solve the nation's cost problem." When confronted with details about how the uninsured were to be covered or how costs would be contained, the support for these options changed markedly. Poll results on any given goal, in isolation, give us no information about how people would actually weigh trade-offs among valued goals and among alternative means to achieving those goals. While there have, in fact, been efforts to develop polls that confront people with trade-offs, those polls have to provide a great deal of information to the respondents for the questions to make sense.[27] As a result, these polls are no longer measuring the actual opinions and knowledge of an inattentive and uninformed public; rather, they are assessing something that begins to approximate what the public *would think,* given a better opportunity to consider the questions at issue. In that respect, telephone polls which pose trade-offs, "informed polling" as it is sometimes called, are a step in the direction of the more ambitious experiment I shall discuss later: deliberative polling. Instead of just being asked questions on the telephone, under deliberative polling randomly chosen respondents in a national sample will gather in a single place where, for several days, they can interact under conditions facilitating sustained deliberation. Such efforts produce very different results from conventional polls, for they create a microcosm of an engaged and informed public.

PARTICIPATION

Polls, whether conventional or deliberative, involve only tiny samples of the public. A properly conducted national random sample will be statistically representative of the entire country. In that sense, it embodies the condition of political equality discussed earlier. A random sample is statistically representative, and each person's opinions count in the same way. Admittedly, conventional polls, even of random samples, do not serve our second value—deliberation. But there is also a third condition we posited earlier, a condition all polls routinely neglect—participation.

Even if a sample were perfectly representative, there is a difference between a sample of several hundred speaking for the nation and the entire citizenry actually speaking for itself. The difference is not so much in the substance of what the people say. With modern random samples, we can know a great deal about the chances that our sample is giving us the same results as those we would have gotten had we asked the entire population. Rather, participation in the political process serves an independent legitimating function. It has sometimes been taken as a form of tacit consent to the authorities that govern us.[28] Or, as Judith Shklar has argued, it is *an affirmation of belonging*.[29] It is a form of connectedness to the system that expresses our collective political identity.

From this perspective, low voter turnouts are a worrisome symptom. They indicate a disconnection from the system and from its shared political identity, a disconnection that is distinguishable from any specific political effects in one election or another. The problem is an old one. Hamilton complained about it in *Federalist* no. 61, noting the "alarming indifference discoverable in the exercise of so valuable a privilege." He speculated that there was a certain threshold of inconvenience that produced nonvoting ("when the place of election is at an inconvenient distance from the elector, the effect upon his conduct will be the same whether that distance be twenty miles or twenty thousand miles"). His insight into the connection between inconvenience and nonparticipation places the discussion squarely within the calculations of individual costs and benefits we encountered earlier in the issue of rational ignorance. Such calculations also illustrate the low level of commitment of the electorate. If voting were a matter of principle, or of great urgency, minor inconveniences would not be decisive. Collectively, the right to vote has, in fact, been a matter of fundamental principle. But individually, it has long been the plaything of convenience.

American voter turnouts are notoriously low by world standards. Even for presidential elections, we are lucky if over half of the citizens of voting age participate. Most European countries routinely have turnouts that are 50 percent higher.[30] Similarly, American turnout levels a hundred years ago were also routinely 50 or 60 percent higher, calculated, of course, for an electorate that was restricted by race and gender. Do such low turnouts make a difference?

From the standpoint of specific elections, there is a great deal of controversy. [Some analysts have established that on many issues, there is no substantive difference between voters and nonvoters.[31] If voters and nonvoters have the same preferences, then participation by the nonvoters would not have been likely to alter the outcome. On the other hand, since nonvoters tend disproportionately to be the less educated and less well-off, there are occasionally dramatic differences.] Frances Fox Piven and Richard Cloward argue, for example, that "the Reagan victory of 1980 was literally made possible by large-scale nonvoting. Just as polls showed that voters tilted toward Reagan by 52 percent over Carter's 38 percent, so did nonvoters tilt toward Carter by 51 percent over 37 percent."[32]

Apart from influence over the outcome, the nonparticipation has an effect on the kind of "mandate" that can plausibly be claimed from the result. Participation is, in other words, centrally connected to our basic question of "When do the people speak?" If too few decide to participate, then the elections are far more tenuously taken as expressions of the voice of the people. In spite of the talk of mandates in the historic 1994 mid-term elections—in which the Republicans took control of Congress—the 39 million voters who favored Republicans and the 35 million voters who favored Democrats were far outnumbered by the 112 million Americans who were eligible to vote but stayed home.

The 1994 mid-term elections offered one of the most explicit attempts to claim a mandate. A Contract with America was published in *TV Guide* and announced with great fanfare. After the Republican victory, Newt Gingrich, the Speaker-to-be, confirmed that the contract would be read aloud every day in the House during the first hundred days of the new session. But even after a month of intense postelection coverage, polls found little public familiarity with the contract. The *New York Times* noted, in summarizing the results of its poll, a month after the election, "Although Mr. Gingrich has been waving around his copy of the Contract with America, which was printed in TV Guide, 72 percent of those polled said they had not read or heard anything about it."[33]

On the other hand, the contract was constructed after intense consultation with polls and focus groups. Hence, the new Speaker could say, correctly, that "If you take a look at the polls and you take a look at the contract, we're pretty much in line with where the country wants to go." When asked, in the same interview on the first day of the new Congress, whether he had any advice for the Democrats on how to adjust to their new minority status, the Speaker offered, "Listen to the American people."[34] Polls have become an essential currency of American politics. They even might be said to offer a kind of "virtual representation" for nonvoters. If legislators follow polls, and if the polls represent everyone, including those who choose not to participate, then the people who are apparently left out have, nevertheless, a means for expressing their preferences. There are, however, so many reasons to question the adequacy of the preferences offered by polls, particularly on complex questions of public policy, that this "representation" of the entire electorate offers small consolation for those concerned with low turnout.

Walter Dean Burnham has ranked the forty-two American presidential elections held between 1828 and 1992 in terms of the percentage of the potential electorate who voted for the winner. (These are all the presidential elections since the advent of the modern party system.) The Reagan victory in 1980, which Vice President–Elect Bush declared to be a "mandate" for no less than seven major propositions ("a mandate for peace and freedom . . . a mandate for prosperity . . . a mandate for opportunity for all Americans . . . a mandate for leadership that is strong and compassionate . . ."), might plausibly be interpreted as no mandate at all. Reagan received votes from only 28 percent of the eligible electorate, which tied his opponent Jimmy Carter's equally slim mandate in 1976, both ranking thirty-sixth out of the forty-two cases. The slimmest mandate of all was Bill Clinton's in 1992. He received only 24.5 percent of the eligible electorate, narrowly beating Woodrow Wilson in 1912 for the lowest percentage in American history.[35] As turnout rates decline, receiving a mere plurality of the half of those who decide to vote is bound to lead to percentages in the range of only a quarter or less of the eligible citizen population. Can a president claim a mandate if three-quarters or more of the citizens who could have voted for him or her did not?

Of course, voting does not exhaust the opportunities for political participation. But participation in its other common forms—writing or phoning a Congressman, making a political contribution, attending a meeting, working for a party or a candidate—engage the electorate at levels that vary between 5 and 10 percent, as compared to about half of the electorate that participates in voting, at least in presidential election years.[36] These other, less-common forms of participation raise difficult issues in interpreting when the people speak.

Senators and congressmen routinely cite the number of phone calls, letters, and faxes they receive on a given issue. They cite these communications as evidence of public opinion among their constituents. Yet they are citing small, self-selected groups who feel strongly enough to commit their energies or resources to a given candidate, issue, or party. Because these are not random samples, it remains difficult to interpret the degree to which the opinions of such small numbers represent broader constituencies. As *Roll Call* notes, "A Senate office that gets 2,000 calls thinks it's being deluged, but the average Senator has five million constituents."[37] Of course, sometimes the mass public does get energized. There is a new breed of lobbyist that mobilizes public opinion to affect congressional votes—by "seizing on unformed public sentiment, marshaling local interest groups and raining faxes, phone calls and letters on Congress or the White House on a few days' notice." Such lobbyists use sophisticated telephone banks to "phone potentially irate citizens, deliver detailed briefings and then transfer the newly aggravated callers directly to the office of the relevant senator or representative."[38]

Political operatives in Congress and the White House sometimes have difficulty distinguishing the apparently spontaneous mobilizations, as in the Zoë Baird case, from those orchestrated by paid lobbyists. Both have become common forms of political participation.

Orchestrated petitions are nothing new. In the early mobilization of Parliament against the king in the 1640s, members of Parliament circulated petitions themselves, even though the petitions purported to be spontaneous initiatives from the people. Samuel Butler satirized this well-known practice:

> The Parliament drew up petitions
> to itself, and sent them, like commissions,
> to well-affected persons, down
> in every city and great town
> with pow'r to levy horse and men,
> only to bring them back again.[39]

AVOIDING TYRANNY: THE ENERGY THAT
REFORGES DEMOCRACY

Participation, political equality, deliberation. We have not yet completed our brief tour of key democratic values. There is one more to be considered. We shall find it in the political thought of the American Founders; we shall find it running throughout the long history of democratic theory and discussion. Perhaps the best expression of its force can be found in the "mental experiment" posed by the economist Joseph Schumpeter, writing about democracy in 1942, a time in which the full horrors of the tyranny of the majority were beginning to become known in the Holocaust unleashed by Nazi Germany.

"Let us transport ourselves into a hypothetical country," he suggests, "that, in a democratic way, practices the persecution of Christians, the burning of witches, and the slaughtering of Jews. We should certainly not approve of these practices on the ground that they have been decided on according to the rules of democratic procedure." There are, Schumpeter concludes, "ideals and interests which the most ardent democrat will put above democracy." To hold to the results of the democratic method would not make sense in such cases: "No doubt one might conceivably hold that, however criminal or stupid . . . the will of the people must prevail," but the very fact that the people have come to such decisions changes our view of the legitimacy of their democratic expression. When the people arrive at such conclusions, "It seems much more natural to speak of the rabble instead of the people and to fight its criminality or stupidity by all the means at one's command."[40]

Tyranny of the majority offers a frightening spectacle to advocates of democracy. We could satisfy all our other conditions—the people could speak through their own participation, votes could be counted so as to satisfy political equality, the issues could be fully debated so as to satisfy deliberation. Still, the system could result in consequences that destroy the rights or the essential interests or the liberties of some

portion of the population, even when the imposition of these deprivations was entirely avoidable. Tyranny of the majority delegitimates the
voice of the people. It takes away the moral claim of that voice to our
allegiance. It invites resistance and protest rather than acceptance. We
shall find that the moral energy that periodically reforges American
democracy comes principally from this fourth condition. The voice of
the people is energized to correct tyranny. This was the rallying cry of
the American Revolution and the founding of the country. It was also
the dominant issue during the second extraordinary transformation of
the American system, Reconstruction, when the tyranny of slavery
began to be corrected. And the third great change, the New Deal,
which fundamentally transformed American society and many elements of the Constitutional system, was directed at injustices and deprivations felt during the Great Depression. Later I shall explore the
notion of Constitutional Moments, in which the people are engaged to
reform their system.[41] The moral energy of the Constitutional Moments our country has thus far experienced has come from this fourth
condition—avoiding tyranny.

Fear of majority tyranny animated the American Founders in their
design. A great deal of their emphasis on deliberation was motivated
by a desire to refine and enlarge public views that might otherwise
lead to unwise decisions. Furthermore, their lack of enthusiasm for
popular participation was due precisely to the fear that the masses
might be aroused in dangerous factions, adverse to the rights of others.
The Founders were also aware that even when the condition of deliberation was met, the masses were capable of dangerous passions. They
took care to distinguish the "democracies" of ancient Greece from the
"republic" they were proposing. The mass public, when aroused, can
do dangerous things adverse to the rights of others.

The Framers had recently lived through Shay's Rebellion. In 1786 a
group of farmers in western Massachusetts demanded debtor relief and
changes in the court system. They armed themselves but were put down
by the state militia. Rumors spread that "the Shaysites had intended to

march on Boston, loot the Bank of Massachusetts, and then march southward redistributing property." The whole episode came to be viewed as exemplifying the dangers and excesses of popular democracy.[42]

The Framers had a significant problem. Nothing similar to the system they were proposing had ever been tried. They were designing an "extended republic" that would operate over a large territory and population. They recognized that their experiment was bold and might set an example for the rest of the world. "But why is the experiment of an extended republic to be rejected merely because it may comprise what is new?" Hamilton asks in *Federalist* no. 14. "Is it not the glory of the people of America that, whilst they have paid a decent regard to the opinions of former times and other nations, they have not suffered a blind veneration for antiquity, for custom or for names to overrule the suggestions of their own good sense?" Hamilton reminds his readers that the Revolutionary War was, itself, unprecedented and that had they waited for precedents, they would still be under the rule of the British monarch.

The issue that made the proposed Constitution novel was the notion that a form of self-government could take place over such a large society without the excesses of popular rule, the "mischiefs of faction," as Madison put it in his famous *Federalist* no. 10, by which he meant "a number of citizens . . . who are united and actuated by some common impulse of passion, or of interest, adverse to the rights of other citizens or to the permanent and aggregate interests of the community." The mischiefs of faction are, of course, synonymous with majority tyranny. It was in this number of the *Federalist* that "Publius" made the argument that tyranny of the majority would be *less* likely in a large or "extended republic" than in a small one.

Madison proposes two very different strategies for "curing" the mischiefs of faction: "removing its causes" and "controlling its effects." The difficulty with the first strategy is that as long as there is liberty, there will be the differences in society that give rise to factions—religious and political differences, differences in property and interest. "Liberty is to faction as air is to fire," but as Madison notes, just as it would be "folly" to get rid of air because it can help produce fire, it would be folly to get rid of liberty because it can help produce faction. Hence Madison turns to controlling the effects of faction.

Madison here offers a number of arguments that the effects of faction are more easily controlled in an "extended republic" than in a small one. "As each representative will be chosen by a greater number of citizens," Madison argues, in a large republic, "it will be more difficult for unworthy candidates to practice with success the vicious arts by which elections are too often carried." Hence, there will be a likelihood that the more worthy candidates will be elected. In Madison's time, the press was undeveloped. Literacy was limited, and the revolution in newspaper manufacturing did not come until the steam-powered presses of the 1830s and electricity in the 1890s. The late 1880s also brought cheaper paper, which permitted the further spread of the mass-circulation daily newspaper.[43] Given these later developments, it is arguable that Madison's speculation that the "vicious arts" of campaigning would be more difficult to practice in a large state than a small one might have to be revised. With the mass media, the vicious arts might even be better practiced to large masses, disconnected as the people are from opportunities for face-to-face political discussion. With the rise of the mass media, Madison's first argument for the large republic takes on a troubling resonance. We cannot imagine what he would have thought of negative campaigning as we have come to know it—with thirty-second spots, sound bites, push polls, and commercials where one candidate "morphs" into another.[44]

Madison's most important argument, however, stands the test of time a good deal better. When the society is small, there will be "fewer distinct parties and interests," and a combination that oppresses the rights of some will be easier to form and maintain. However, "extend the sphere and you take in a greater variety of parties and interests; you make it less probable that a majority of the whole will have a common motive to invade the rights of other citizens; or if such a common motive exists, it will be more difficult for all who feel it to discover their own strength and to act in unison with each other."

The factions will be more numerous, and they will counteract one another. Given the separation of powers, "ambition must be made to counteract ambition," as Madison says in *Federalist* no. 51. The extended republic proposed by the Founders can resist tyranny because power is not concentrated and the factions are likely to cancel each other out.

I have not yet defined *tyranny,* whether of the majority or, conceivably, of the minority. The Founders argued against the backdrop of an eighteenth-century consensus on God-given natural rights. Hence the political scientist Robert Dahl's gloss on the Madisonian definition of tyranny: "every severe deprivation of a natural right."[45] The difficulty is that we need to confront the issue of majority tyranny during periods where such a consensus has dissolved. Let us say rather that tyranny occurs when there is an avoidable severe deprivation, and let us mean by a severe deprivation the denial of a person or group's most basic rights or fundamental interests. What interests are taken as fundamental, what rights are taken as most basic, will vary from one context or period to another. But for us to call an act tyranny, we would need to establish a claim that someone's most basic rights or interests had been sacrificed.

I say "avoidable" severe deprivation because there may be instances where no matter what is done, someone's fundamental interests will be sacrificed. And by avoidable, I mean that a policy is chosen when there is an alternative policy that would not also have imposed severe deprivations on anyone. If there is a natural disaster and only one of two groups, A or B, can be rescued, it is not tyrannous to rescue just one. If both were left to perish, that would be objectionable. However, if there were earlier, foreseeable decisions that could have laid the groundwork for rescuing both, there might be a further argument. But at the point of decision, avoidable deprivations provide a workable basis for an understanding of tyranny.[46]

SMALL-SCALE DEMOCRACY

If we look at the four democratic conditions—political equality, deliberation, participation and non-tyranny—contemporary American practices leave much to be desired. As should become increasingly clear, it is difficult to institutionalize all four simultaneously, at least for the large nation-state. We can certainly make progress on each. But as fundamental goals they tend to conflict, one with another. As we open up opportunities for participation and political equality for the entire citizenry, for example, we create incentives for rational ignorance that destroy deliberation. We shall also sometimes create the conditions feared by the Founders in which passions of the masses are aroused that are adverse to the interests of some minority. We cannot view the history of referendums, for example, in some of our western states without rekindling some of these worries.[47] On the other hand, if we reinstitute deliberation among elites, or among self-selected groups, we undermine political equality and participation in the nation as a whole.

At the small scale, however, it is far easier to see how at least some of these values can be realized simultaneously. In ancient Athens, for instance, there was a high degree of political equality, deliberation, and participation, at least among citizens. Mogens Hansen summarizes the system of citizen rotation for juries, legislative commissions, and membership in the most important decision-making body, the Council, all chosen by lottery or random selection:

> The rule that a man could be a councillor no more than twice in a lifetime means that every second citizen above thirty, i.e. something like every third citizen, served at least once as a member of the Council, and three quarters of all councillors in any one year had to serve for a night and a day as *epistates ton prytaneon* [essentially, president of Athens]. . . . Simple calculation leads to this astounding result: *every fourth adult male Athenian could say, "I have been for twenty-four hours President of Athens"* (emphasis added).[48]

Given that between one-fifth and one-tenth of the citizenry participated in any one meeting of the Assembly, and given that the Assembly met between thirty and forty times a year, the percentage of the citizenry engaged in serious political participation was truly remarkable. Furthermore, the extensive discussion in the Assembly, where every citizen had the right to speak, and the careful deliberative processes in the citizens' juries and legislative commissions and in the Council would have produced an admirable degree of deliberation. Indeed, any citizen in the Assembly had to worry that he could later be prosecuted for an "illegal proposal"—which meant basically that if his proposal was judged unwise by a later citizen's jury, he could face serious penalties. The fact that juries could, in effect, override or undo decisions taken in the Assembly demonstrates the legitimacy the Athenians ascribed to representation by lot. The juries and commissions of five hundred or more were deliberative microcosms of the entire citizenry. Because their memberships were chosen by lot they satisfied our criterion of political equality. Because the opportunities to serve on such bodies were widely distributed through rotation, they served the causes of participation as well as political equality. While there is some evidence that the jury membership was sometimes skewed by age and class, the introduction of pay eventually made the juries reasonable microcosms of the citizenry.

Hence, although Athens is usually invoked as the birthplace of direct democracy, some of our key aspirations were fulfilled through devices of representation. Some of these same devices would be extremely useful in a modern context.

Yet the democracy of ancient Athens had its defects, as the American Founders took pains to remind us. The reputation of Athens has suffered for two and a half millennia because the Athenians killed Socrates. Furthermore, by modern standards, the citizenry was so restricted that many suffered tyranny by their very status—women, metics (free noncitizens with no political rights), and slaves. Clearly, there is an element of truth in Madison's argument that some of our democratic aspirations may better be realized in a large or extended republic rather than in a small-scale democracy.

Depending on the social conditions, however, there may well be small-scale versions of democracy that do better on all our criteria. Northern New Mexico and southern Colorado have long hosted more than a thousand cooperative communities built around ancient irrigation systems called acequias. Many of these systems date back to the sixteenth century. These acequias are not only water supply systems, they are also long-functioning direct democracies. Their members, *parcientes,* not only share the work of maintaining the systems, they also share in the decision-making process in open meetings on a stream-by-stream basis. Each member has such a stake in the operation of the local water system, and the communities are so tightly knit, that participation in the work and in the shared decision making is nearly total.

Our four criteria—political equality, deliberation, participation and non-tyranny—are routinely satisfied, but in communities of a few hundred that have been operating in this manner for up to four hundred years. While there are elected administrators (Mayordomos), and while representatives of the acequias may be sent to broader associations, the effective decision making occurs through direct democracy at the local level. Because the well-being of each member depends on the irrigation system, there is no divorce, in the minds of members, between the working of the system and their personal welfare. The two are intrinsically connected, which results in strong incentives for participation and for serious discussion of collective problems.[49]

The acequias seem to live up to the mythic picture of communal participation that Ralph Waldo Emerson made famous in his account of the New England town meeting—where "every opinion had an utterance" and where each person had "his fair weight." In Emerson's description of this "real" version of the ideal social compact, no action is taken "without the whole population of this town having a voice in the affair."[50] Emerson's ideal image fulfills all our criteria simultaneously.

But studies of real New England town meetings, contemporary or historical, show considerable variation in levels of participation and in their representativeness. Jane Mansbridge, for example, studied a Vermont town, "Selby," in some depth. She found incentives for disproportionate participation for the "old-timers, the villagers, the elderly, the middle class, and the self-confident." Although Selby demonstrated a high level of participation by American standards for local issues—66 percent—it is a level that nevertheless falls far short of democratic ideals for small-group democracy. Some New England towns have, historically, had participation rates of about half that level, Mansbridge notes.[51] Even at the small scale, meaningful democracy is a tenuous creation.

THE FOUNDERS' VISION

The American Founders did not seek to realize all four of the values we have identified here. Although they sought implementation of deliberation and non-tyranny, they were somewhat wary of both political equality and participation. It was the anti-Federalists who initially championed the latter two values and inserted them into the continuing American debate.

Concerned with the difficulties of controlling factions in a "pure democracy," the small, direct democracy of the ancients, Madison advocated a "republic" that would be based on "successive filtrations" of the public views. At the Constitutional Convention, he endorsed the popular election of only one branch of the legislature, the House of Representatives, because "the great fabric to be raised would be more stable and durable if it should rest on the solid foundation of the people themselves." But this popular foundation was to be refined through "the policy of . . . successive filtrations."[52] The people's voice was to be filtered or refined by the deliberations of representatives. As he later explained in *Federalist* no. 10, "The delegation of the government" to elected representatives would serve to "refine and enlarge the public views by passing them through a chosen body of citizens." Because such representatives would be able to resist "temporary or partial considerations," Madison argues: "It may well happen that the public voice, pronounced by the representatives of the people, will be more consonant to the public good than if pronounced by the people themselves, convened for the purpose."

It is not that Madison has an unrealistically optimistic picture of elected representatives. As we saw earlier, he refers in the same number of the *Federalist* to the "vicious arts by which elections are too often carried." But in a large republic, such practices will be made more difficult, he believes, and in any case, "ambition can be made to counteract ambition."

Hamilton also expressed a clear sense of how popular opinion would have to be resisted by representatives engaged in deliberation. "The republican principle demands that the deliberative sense of the community should govern," he declared in *Federalist* no. 71, but this sense may be quite different from what the people themselves think at any given time: "It does not require an unqualified complaisance to every sudden breeze of passion or to every transient impulse which the people may receive from the arts of men, who flatter their prejudices to betray their interests."

The central virtue of the Senate, for Hamilton, is that because its members were *indirectly* elected they were, by design, in a position to resist the immediate expressions of public opinion: "When occasions present themselves in which the interests of the people are at variance with their inclinations, it is the duty of the persons whom they have appointed to be the guardians of those interests to withstand the temporary delusion in order to give them time and opportunity for more cool and sedate reflection."

The point of successive filtrations is to insulate the deliberative process from the immediate views of the people. The entire construction is at one remove (or more) from popular participation. It is also not directed at achieving political equality. Indeed, Madison's central metaphor that representation is to refine and enlarge the public views can be taken as meaning *refinement* in the sense of arriving at the best quality—the elite, in other words—of the society.[53] As Stanley Elkins and Eric McKitrick note about the authors of the *Federalist:* "The world in which they all functioned was hardly a 'democratic' world . . . but an elite one." While the people had an important role at the base of the new Constitution, "The peoples' virtue was still primarily to be thought of as their capacity less to act than to choose wisely, 'to obtain for rulers,' as Madison put it in Number 57, 'men who possess most wisdom to discern and most virtue to pursue the common good.' "[54] The representatives were in many ways the elite of the society destined for public service, who would be capable of resisting the "temporary delusions" of public opinion. Precisely because of their superior virtue and wisdom, it was thought that they could better deliberate for the whole of society.

As the historian Douglass Adair has argued, Madison took the idea of a system of indirect elections from David Hume's "Idea of a Perfect Commonwealth." It was this idea that permitted Madison to argue, contrary to Montesquieu, that a large state might have advantages in dealing with factions. Madison's crucial metaphor of refining the public views can be found in Hume:

> In a large government . . . there is compass and room enough to *refine the democracy,* from the lower people, who may be admitted into the first elections or first concoction of the commonwealth, to the higher magistrates, who direct all the movements. At the same time, the parts are so distant and remote, that it is very difficult, either by intrigue, prejudice or passion, to hurry them into any measures against the public interest (emphasis added).[55]

In Madison's early statement of the theory that was to become central to the Framer's Constitution, "Notes on the Confederacy," he outlined the function of indirect elections as one of filtering and refining to achieve an elite capable of deliberation. He specified "such a process of elections as will most certainly extract from the mass of the Society the purest and noblest characters which it contains; such as will at once feel most strongly the proper motives to pursue the end of their appointment, and be most capable to devise the proper means of attaining it."[56]

But this whole structure of indirect elections and successive filtrations of public opinion—for example, having a Senate chosen by state legislatures and a president chosen by a freely deliberating Electoral College—was to be challenged, and progressively abandoned, by the overwhelming direction of democratic reform in the United States since the Founding. As our system has become more direct, through both formal and informal changes, there is less "filtering" of the public views by elites—and, generally, a good deal less deliberation. Our effective dismantling of some of the mechanisms specified by the Founders has had effects that would not have surprised them. The dismantling was accomplished largely in the name of democracy and with good intentions. But democracy comes in many and conflicting forms.

THE ANTI-FEDERALIST DISSENT

The opening salvos in the struggle over the Founders' elite democracy began at once, in the debates with the anti-Federalists. Many of their attacks on the new Constitution can be summarized as charges that the proposed plan neglected two of our four values—political equality and participation.

The anti-Federalist writer Brutus attacked the plan for the House of Representatives on grounds that "the distance between the people and their representatives will be so very great, that there is no probability that a farmer, however respectable, will be chosen—the mechanics of every branch must expect to be excluded from a seat in the Body—It will and must be esteemed a station too high and exalted to be filled by any but the first men in the state, in point of fortune." Brutus feared that only "the natural aristocracy of the country" would be elected. The result would be a representative body too elitist to have any connection to public opinion: "The well born and highest orders of life, as they term themselves, will be ignorant of the sentiments of the middling class of citizens, strangers to their abilities, wants, and difficulties." We would have a "representation" that was "merely nominal— a mere burlesque."[57]

The House was, of course, the most democratic of the proposed institutions. These same arguments were applied even more strongly to the proposed Senate, the Judiciary, and other offices. The anti-Federalists believed that these bodies would be filled with what they called, using John Adams's words, "the few, the well-born." "Common people" cannot fill such offices, a "Federal Farmer" argued, because "an expensive education is required."[58]

Similarly, the anti-Federalist minority report from the Pennsylvania Convention argued that the representation of interests would necessarily be inadequate "because the sense and views of 3 or 4 millions of people diffused over so extensive a territory comprising such various climates, products, habits and interests and opinions cannot be collected in so small a body." The resulting unrepresentative body would be elitist. "Men of the most elevated rank in life will alone be chosen," the anti-Federalists complained. "The other orders in the society, such as farmers, traders and mechanics, who all ought to have a competent number of their best informed men in the legislature, will be totally underrepresented."[59]

The anti-Federalists sought a system that was closer to the people. They wanted short terms, rotation in office, and the influence of the people and their views brought directly to bear on government. They were suspicious of the separation of powers, which they viewed as an impediment to the popular will, and of the entire apparatus of successive filtration constructed by the Framers. The inventions the Federalists viewed as serving deliberation were viewed by the anti-Federalists as entrenchments of aristocratic privilege impeding the popular will.

"Centinel," a leading anti-Federalist writer, advocated simple government and a unicameral legislature. His position was attacked by the Federalists for ignoring the fact that the separation of powers was meant to promote deliberation: "The sole intention of [the separation] is to produce wise and mature deliberation." The idea is to prevent "rash and hasty decisions."[60]

Anti-Federalists also advocated frequent elections and rotation in office. They constantly criticized the long terms proposed in the Constitution for both the House and the Senate. They declared annual elections to be the solution, along with possible provisions for rotation in office.[61]

The anti-Federalist vision was generally that there be a small, simple government close to the people, with frequent elections and, to the extent that representation was necessary, it should mirror the entire citizenry. In these respects, the anti-Federalists deemphasized the aristocratic deliberation of the Founders' Constitution by promoting the popular values of political equality and participation.

Of course, the anti-Federalists lost the initial battle. But it is arguable that crucial elements of their vision, in the hands of later champions, actually triumphed in the rise of what I call "mass democracy." The *elite democracy* of the Founders, which emphasized deliberation and non-tyranny but downplayed both political equality and participation, has given way in successive battles and innovations to a form of democracy that attempts to promote political equality and participation—often at the expense of deliberation and non-tyranny. We shall call this variant mass democracy.

The most striking vulnerability of mass democracy is that it neglects one of the values emphasized by the Founders—deliberation. Mass democracy provides numerous opportunities for public consultation, both formal and informal, but it does not provide any institutional mechanisms that motivate mass deliberation. The central and recurring problem facing democratic reform is whether it will ever prove possible to achieve all four values simultaneously.

Let us call a system that achieved all four of these values simultaneously a *democracy of civic engagement*. As we shall see, a great deal of change, both formal and informal, can be summarized as being part of the transition from the elite democracy of the Founders to mass democracy. Will it be possible to make the transition from mass democracy to one that is civically engaged in its ability to fulfill all four values?

While our four democratic conditions can sometimes be achieved simultaneously in small-scale situations, they are harder to realize on a large scale. Although there are things we can do to further each of these values, it is often the case that furthering one will have an adverse effect on the others. Instead of a unified and coherent ideal in which these valued parts fit together in a single clear vision of what we should be striving for, we have conflicting values, each of which takes policy making and political reform in a different direction.

I term this situation "ideals without an ideal" because there is no single ideal vision to be progressively realized.[62] Rather there are conflicting portions of the ideal picture, and emphasis on each would take us in a different direction. This situation is not unique to democratic reform but applies to many political conflicts and policy choices. It is part of what makes hard choices hard—requiring that a political system have a capacity somewhere for deliberation about conflicting values, conflicting visions.

3

HOW "PUBLIC OPINION" BECAME
THE VOICE OF THE PEOPLE

"LIKE A BURGLAR":
INFORMAL PROCESSES OF REFORM

Many of the crucial changes in the American system have come, not
through legislation or through Constitutional amendments, but
through *informal* changes in democratic expectations—unofficial
changes in the commonly accepted notions about how people should
act in order to fulfill a given role. Consider how changing notions of
democracy have affected the Electoral College, the national party conventions, and the process for selecting U.S. senators. In each case
what the Founders had envisioned as a deliberative body—to allow
for face-to-face discussion among those who were elected—eventually became a group whose members received instructions directly
from voters. In each case, the deliberators became messengers once
the effective locus of decision was moved closer to the people. After
elective results were sanctified as the "voice of the people," it became
hard for contrary decisions to withstand the moral and political force
that seemed to be behind those results.

It comes as a surprise to many Americans to learn that the Electoral
College was originally intended as a deliberative body. As Hamilton
explained the system for choosing presidents in *Federalist* no. 68:

"The immediate election should be made by men most capable of analyzing the qualities adapted to the station and acting under circumstances favorable to deliberation." The idea was that the great mass of the public would not know the characters and qualifications of candidates. As one historian summarized that concern, it reflected "a conviction that the extent of the country and the difficulty of communication did not permit informed selection of a national candidate."[1] One can only wonder what the Founders would have thought of our process today, in which electors serve merely as proxies for a direct vote of the people on a state-by-state basis. Both the extent of the country and the effectiveness of communications have increased unimaginably. It is still arguable, however, that the Federalists' worries about the difficulty of the public's making an "informed choice" of president were well-founded.

Instead of the public at large, Hamilton argued in *Federalist* no. 62, "a small number of persons, selected by their fellow citizens from the general mass, will be most likely to possess the information and discernment requisite to so complicated an investigation." Hence the initial hopes for the Electoral College.

The idea that members of the Electoral College would "investigate" the merits of the competing candidates, and discuss them together (meeting on a state-by-state basis), raises the specter of what we now call faithless electors, who betray the people's will by voting against the popular votes in their states. The original notion, that electors would seriously deliberate, was clearly a key part of the scheme of successive filtrations, which would pass popular opinion through the deliberations of chosen representatives. This indirect process was prized by the founders as a bulwark against the temporary inclinations and delusions of an aroused public. But as Henry Jones Ford, back in 1898, summarized the transformation during the first century of the system's operation, "Public opinion suppressed the constitutional discretion of the electoral college, and made it a register of the popular vote as taken by the states."[2] The situation has not changed since. The

Electoral College worked exactly as originally envisioned by the Founders for only one candidate, George Washington. As the institution has developed, the gains in popular control have had to be balanced against the loss in deliberation.[3] As things developed the democratic idea of popular control left no discretionary room for elites to impose their view of the best candidate. Without any change in the Constitution, the system was quickly transformed to conform to a different democratic vision, one closer to popular decision.

The Electoral College is now treated as a vestigial remain of an earlier stage of our political evolution. Like an appendix, it once played an essential role. And like an appendix, it can sometimes produce a crisis. If a candidate wins by small margins in some states in the popular vote and loses by big margins in others, it is still possible for that candidate to be elected by the Electoral College while losing the popular vote. This has happened at least twice, in 1876 and 1888. In other cases, deadlock in the electoral college can throw the election into the House of Representatives, as occurred in 1800 and 1824. The modern prospects for this kind of crisis are especially likely in a genuine three-way race that denies any candidate a majority in the Electoral College. Such a possibility seemed seriously to threaten for a time in 1992 with the Perot candidacy. It will certainly recur.

In the first years of the Republic, most states did not even hold a popular vote for president. Rather, the legislatures selected the presidential electors, just as they selected senators. Both votes were part of the successive filtration of public opinion envisioned by the Founders. It was not until 1824 that eighteen of the country's twenty-four states held a popular vote. Only then did it become meaningful to talk about the "people" voting for president on a national basis.

After Washington's two elections, the rise of the Congressional caucus system for nominating presidential candidates created a party line-up for the general election that effectively destroyed the Founders' original mechanism of presidential selection. No longer could anyone credibly claim that members of the Electoral College would simply choose the single most meritorious individual. Party politics played out in the state selections of electors. The candidate endorsed by the party caucus became, in effect, the national leader of the party.

In some ways, the caucus system offered yet another flawed embodiment of our ideal of face-to-face democracy adapted to the large nation state. Even though many political deals were made, it was nevertheless true that elected representatives of the people (members of Congress) met in a room and deliberated on which candidate to select. As the system was dying in the 1820s it was even defended on the grounds that "it was a tried method that offered the best expression of nationwide rather than simply sectional interest."[4] The caucus was, in effect, an elected, representative body that could meet in one room and make a decision on nominating a party's candidate for president on a national basis. But this profoundly elitist method was clearly ripe for democratization. It was tied too closely to political deals in Washington and machinations of members of Congress. The national party convention made its appearance in 1831 as a way of directing the voice of the people more directly to the selection of presidential candidates. These national party conventions faced, in turn, a similar process of democratization.

The same basic process of supplanting elite deliberations with mass decisions eventually played itself out with the national party conventions. We have not had a multi-ballot convention on the Democratic side since 1952 or on the Republican side since 1948. The Democrats took 46 ballots to nominate Woodrow Wilson in 1912. They needed 103 roll calls over seventeen days to nominate John W. Davis in 1924.[5] Now such convention battles seem historic curiosities, legacies from a different system, whose operation has long since lapsed in the face of popular control. The national party conventions have become largely media pep rallies, orchestrated in the name of party unity. Apparently spontaneous demonstrations are often scripted to the minute for prime-time television viewing. The drama of real deliberation is avoided because it might give the appearance of disunity, risking giving the wrong impression to a national television audience.

After 1968, when Hubert Humphrey won the Democratic nomination without entering a single primary, a wave of reform democratized the system, encouraging primaries as the selection procedure for delegates to the national party conventions. The number of states holding primaries went from seventeen in 1968 to thirty-nine in 1992. The reformers saw the national party conventions as smoke-filled rooms where political deals were cut. It is ironic that the first of the commissions in this major wave of reform, the McGovern-Fraser Commission, offered as the principal argument for *retaining* the national party conventions the idea that the "face-to-face confrontation of Democrats of every persuasion in a periodic mass meeting is productive of healthy debate." Collecting delegates from all over the country in a single (large) room embodied our ideal of face-to-face democratic deliberation. However, the principal effect of the commission's prescription—"the cure for the ills of democracy is more democracy"—was the proliferation of primaries, which tied the hands of elected delegates and emptied the process of deliberation.

Primaries placed the locus of decision in the hands of the voters rather than their elected representatives. For better or worse, the democratic reforms gave the conventions a great deal less to decide because they created a situation where the most important decisions would be made by others long before the convention gathered together. Just as members of the Electoral College quickly became messengers rather than deliberators, once the public will was clear based on a popular vote, so did the delegates to the national party conventions. They became messengers pledged to deliver whatever was decided in their respective primaries.

At first glance, it might seem as if the reform of the U.S. Senate elections followed a different path. There was, of course, an official change, the Seventeenth Amendment to the Constitution, which went into effect in 1913. But the process of informal reform had already brought about much the same result outside of the formal amendment process. Just as the popular vote turned the members of the Electoral College into messengers rather than deliberators, and just as decisions at the state level, whether primaries or state conventions, turned delegates to the national political conventions into messengers rather than deliberators, so too was the process of selecting senators democratized by being brought to the mass public long before the passage of the Seventeenth Amendment.

Initially, it was thought inappropriate for candidates for the U.S. Senate to campaign. Indeed, the Lincoln-Douglas debates, in which each candidate was backed by a slate of state legislators pledged to vote for him for the U.S. Senate, was a crucial moment in reforming the process. The campaign was condemned at the time as inappropriate because it effectively took the choice of a U.S. senator to the voters.

The *Cincinnati Commercial* complained:

It is difficult to conceive of anything more illegitimate. . . . The Senator . . . is the representative . . . of the state, as an independent polity, and not . . . of its individual citizens; and any attempt to forestall the action of the Legislature, either by party action or personal appeal to the people . . . is . . . an offense against the sovereignty whose freedom of action they thereby seek to fetter and control.[6]

Even earlier than the Lincoln-Douglas debates, which captured the imagination of the entire nation through press accounts, there had been public canvasses for the Senate in many states. As early as 1834 in Mississippi, nonbinding votes were taken to advise the state legislature on party nominations for U.S. Senate. This process was formalized with the development of the direct primary. Primaries for party nominations for U.S. Senate began as early as 1888 in South Carolina. By 1910, twenty-eight states nominated senatorial candidates by party primary.

Primary nominations still did not provide for the will of the people in the general election. However, Oregon developed a system of lining up slates of legislators who would promise to abide by an unofficial public vote in the general election. By 1913 variations of the Oregon system had spread to twenty-nine of the forty-eight states. The voice of the people turned the state legislatures into state versions of the modern Electoral College, at least insofar as the choice of senator was concerned. By the time of the Senate debate on the Seventeenth Amendment, the effective choice had already been given to the public. Senator Cummins of Iowa, a supporter of the change, debated Senator Heyburn of Idaho, a leading opponent, on the floor of the Senate:

MR. CUMMINS: The Senator from Idaho is insisting . . . that if the voters of the United States be permitted to say who shall be their Senators, then this body will be overrun by a crowd of incompetent and unfit and rash and socialistic and radical men who have no proper view of government. I am simply calling to his attention the fact that the people of this country, in despair of amending the Constitution, have accomplished the reform for themselves.

MR. HEYBURN: Like a burglar.

MR. CUMMINS: In an irregular way, I agree, but they have accomplished it.

MR. HEYBURN: Like a burglar.

MR. CUMMINS: And they have accomplished it so effectively that, whether the Constitution is amended or not, the people in many or most of the States will choose their own Senators.[7]

Only a harsh critic would now agree with Senator Heyburn's prediction that the result of voters choosing senators directly would be that "this body will be overrun by a crowd of incompetent and unfit and rash and socialistic and radical men who have no proper view of government." But right or wrong, there has been no turning back once the decision is placed in the hands of the people.

It is striking how much of this major reform could be accomplished without any change in the Constitution, and even without any change in Federal law. As with many other changes, the power of the democratic idea, once the people speak in a credible manner, can be employed to change the norms of behavior in key roles so that when an official change comes, it only ratifies the completed revolution.

BRYCE'S PROPHECY:
GOVERNMENT BY PUBLIC OPINION

When the movement toward popular decision was still far from clear, America was visited by an unusually perceptive British politician and historian named James Bryce (eventually Viscount Bryce of Dechmont and a member of the House of Lords). Bryce published his observations in what has become a classic discussion of America—*The American Commonwealth* (1888).

Bryce's method was eclectic and unorthodox. According to a colleague: "Bryce talked with everybody within reach, or to put it more accurately, he started everybody talking and then listened to them." He probed all strata of society, "on shipboard, on railway trains, in hotel lobbies, with cab drivers on his way from place to place, with the barbers who trimmed his unruly beard, or with the workers in factories or shops which he liked to explore."[8] The result was a prophecy that would have startled the American Founders. It was a prophecy that went largely unnoticed at the time but that, as we shall see, electrified a key democratic reformer a half-century later— George Gallup.

Bryce broke down the development of democracies into four stages, or forms. First, there were the "primary assemblies," the direct democracies of ancient Greece and "those of the early Teutonic tribes, which have survived in a few Swiss cantons." Because the "whole people" had to meet together, "such a system of direct popular government is possible only in small communities," he concluded. It is not relevant to modern democracies and remains "a matter rather of antiquarian curiosity." Here Bryce was identifying the historical—and perhaps mythical—roots of the ideal of face-to-face democracy.[9]

A second form of democracy, according to Bryce, is that dominated by "representative bodies, Parliaments and Chambers." In this system, elected representatives have "a tolerably free hand, leaving them in power for a considerable space of time, and allowing them to act unchecked, except in so far as custom, or possibly some fundamental law, limits their discretion." In this familiar, representative system, the parliament acts in the name of the best interests of the country; it may follow the wishes of the public, "unless it should be convinced that in some particular point it knows better than the majority what the interests of the country require" (268). Bryce was intimately familiar with such a system. He was serving as a member of the British House of Commons at the time he was writing. The extended period of time between elections and the resulting latitude given representatives to vote their conscientious views provide vital insulation from the pressures of public opinion in the major European democracies, in Bryce's view.

The third form of democracy, claimed Bryce, was different from the English model and was, in fact, a distinctively American innovation. It is "something between the other two," in that it combines the direct consultation with the people characteristic of primary assemblies with the election of representatives characteristic of parliamentary democracies. Although there is still a legislature, "It is elected for so short a time and checked in so many ways that much of its power and dignity has departed." Most important, the representatives are "conceived of" differently—"not as wise and strong men chosen to govern, but as delegates under specific orders to be renewed at short intervals" (268).

The key to the American hybrid is the propensity of elected representatives to defer to their impressions of public opinion. This is "the form which naturally produces . . . Government by Public Opinion." By this Bryce means that "the wishes and views of the people prevail, even before they have been conveyed through the regular law-appointed organs and without the need of their being so conveyed" (269).

Bryce describes an absolute monarchy where the merest gesture from the king, the merest hint, or the king's "initial written on a scrap of paper is as sure of obedience as his full name signed on a parchment authenticated by the Great Seal." In Bryce's view, the absolute ruler of the United States is public opinion, and government officials attempt, *informally,* to determine the ruler's wishes and conform: "Where the power of the people is absolute, legislators and administrators are quick to catch its wishes in whatever way they may be indicated, and do not care to wait for the methods which the law prescribes. This happens in America" (269).

Bryce is describing the long-term tendency of American politics toward what he calls "Government by Public Opinion." It is a goal toward which Americans "have marched with steady steps. No other people now stands so near it" (267). In such a system, public opinion is the "key" that will "unlock every door" (264). It is the ultimate source of power: "Towering over Presidents and State governors, over Congress and State legislatures, over conventions and the vast machinery of party, public opinion stands out, in the United States, as the great source of power, the master of servants who tremble before it" (267).

Writing in the 1880s, Bryce saw America as falling into this third stage but tending toward a fourth: "A fourth stage would be reached if the will of the majority of the citizens were to become ascertainable at all times, and without the need of its passing through a body of representatives, possibly even without the need of voting machinery at all" (262).

In the fourth stage, "the sway of public opinion would have become more complete, because more continuous" than in any known countries. "Popular government would have been pushed so far as almost to dispense with, or at any rate to anticipate, the legal modes in which the majority speaks its will at the polling booths" (263). Bryce calls this stage "Rule of public opinion," where the assessment of public opinion is a continuous process. This last stage goes even farther: "for public opinion would not only reign but govern" (263).

At the time he was writing, Bryce admitted that there were "mechanical difficulties" in working out a method of government where public opinion would effectively rule as a continuous presence (263). But he anticipated in general form, if not in its specifics, the eventual influence of public opinion polling and various forms of electronic interaction that try to move us closer to his fourth stage and that make its realization a possibility. Writing before the flowering of the Progressive movement, before the influence of television, computers, and opinion polling, Bryce saw the overwhelming tendency of American politics toward ever more direct and ever more continuous consultation with public opinion. Most astutely, he saw that the informal consultations—the hints from the absolute sovereign, if you will—could be just as powerful as any official act. In this he anticipated the constant attempts by contemporary politicians and commentators to invoke poll results and exit polls, along with phone calls, letters, and faxes, to claim the authority of the "master before whom all tremble."

But what was this public opinion according to Bryce? He was under no illusions about its solidity or its rationality. Conjoined with his predictions, he offered a shrewd description of the slim basis on which public opinion is formed. He asks us to imagine a businessman reading the newspaper in the morning at breakfast: "He reads that Prince Bismarck has announced a policy of protection for German industry, or that Mr. Henry George has been nominated for the mayoralty of New York. These statements arouse in his mind sentiments of approval and disapproval. . . . They also rouse an expectation of certain consequences likely to follow" (251–252).

Our imaginary businessman reading the morning paper is not keenly analyzing consequences. He is not investing much effort in scrutinizing the details of national and international developments. He

receives vague impressions and emotional reactions. Whatever sentiments or expectations he has about the news event, they are *not:*

> based on processes of conscious reasoning—our business man
> has not time to reason at breakfast—they are merely impressions
> formed on the spur of the moment. He turns to the leading article
> in the newspaper, and his sentiments and expectations are con-
> firmed or weakened. . . . He goes down to his office in the train,
> talks there to two or three acquaintances, and perceives that they
> agree or do not agree with his own still faint impressions. (252)

After talking to others, he finds that "the evening paper has collected the opinions of the morning papers"; and he is exposed to the
papers again the next day. Soon, "the opinions of ordinary minds, hitherto fluid and undetermined, has begun to crystallize into a solid
mass." As the debate unfolds, "the effect of controversy is to drive
the partisans on either side from some of their arguments, which
are shown to be weak; to confirm them in others which they think
strong, and to make them take up a definite position on one side"
(252). Eventually, the issue may come before the public and a vote
would be required.

In assessing how such opinions come into being, Bryce concludes:

> In examining the process by which opinion is formed, we cannot
> fail to note how small a part of the view which the average man
> entertains when he goes to vote is really of his own making. His
> original impression was faint and perhaps shapeless; its present
> definiteness and strength are mainly due to what he has heard and
> read. He has been told what to think, and why to think it. Argu-
> ments have been supplied to him from without, and controversy
> has embedded them in his mind. Although he supposes his view
> to be his own, he holds it rather because his acquaintances, his
> newspapers, his party leaders all hold it. His acquaintances do the
> like. (253)

This is not an inspiring picture. Modern views of public opinion, supported by empirical research, confirm Bryce's shrewd observations about the sources of that opinion, and the influence on it of elites and the media, as well as of the inattention of the mass public.[10] By modern standards, Bryce's businessman is actually fairly engaged. Yet there is a sense in which his opinions are not his own and in which he has merely processed vague impressions from the media and from his acquaintances. The accumulated effect of this process on millions of citizens produces the master who towers over our elected leaders and the "key that will unlock any door." The giant who rules America may stand over presidents and senators, but it is constructed from the most ineffable of materials—the casual impressions of ordinary citizens.

GALLUP'S ANSWER

About fifty years after *The American Commonwealth,* a young psychologist and entrepreneur from Iowa based in Princeton, New Jersey, proclaimed and demonstrated to the world that he had pioneered the "solution" to Bryce's "mechanical difficulty" in systematically measuring public opinion. George Gallup was fond of quoting Bryce's account of public opinion at length. In particular, he would cite Bryce on the need for a continuous method for reporting public opinion. Given the expense of referendums, Bryce did not see how his fourth stage, the "rule of public opinion," might actually be reached, even though he saw America's movement toward it. Bryce's prophecy was that America would lead the world in approaching such a system but that there remained "the mechanical difficulties . . . of working such a method" (263).

Bryce admitted that although Switzerland, for instance, had occasional referendums, one question remained: "How, without the greatest inconvenience, can votes be frequently taken on all the chief questions that arise?" Bryce saw government by public opinion as operating informally: "Even where the machinery for weighing or measuring the popular will from week to week or month to month has not been, and is not likely to be, invented, there may nevertheless be a disposition on the part of the rulers . . . *to act as if it existed*" (emphasis added). He envisioned political actors who would "look incessantly for manifestations of current popular opinion and . . . shape their course in according with their reading of those manifestations" (263). No modern reader, aware of the deference now shown to polls on a daily basis by politicians and the media, can read Bryce's words without sensing that here is a prophecy that has come to pass.

Gallup adopted Bryce's vision of democracies that needed ever more *continuous* sources of information about public opinion. He agreed with Bryce that "the action of opinion is continuous, that of voting occasional, and in the intervals between . . . changes may take place materially affecting the views of the voters." Equally, Gallup saw, building on Bryce, there was the problem of interpreting the vote at elections. Voters cast their ballots for candidates, but to what degree were they also voting for what the candidates stood for? "How can we tell whether the public is voting for the man or for his platform? How can we tell whether all the candidate's views are endorsed, or whether some are favored and others opposed by the voters?"[11]

Gallup, for example, noted that President Roosevelt did not make his proposed enlargement of the Supreme Court an issue in the 1936 election. But if he had, he "would undoubtedly have assumed that his reelection had given him a mandate to go ahead with the Court change." Yet Gallup could demonstrate with his new instrument of public opinion surveys that "the majority of voters were against altering the Supreme Court." Gallup saw that the opinion poll could deflate the tendency of candidates to claim a mandate where there might be only a victory.[12]

Gallup had burst on the national scene with his bold challenge to the *Literary Digest* that he could better predict the outcome of the 1936 election with a scientific sample of a few thousand than could the magazine with its returns of millions of cards. The *Digest* had been almost exactly on the mark in 1932, and Gallup could launch his dream of a scientific sample only by giving the subscribing newspapers a money-back guarantee: his prediction would have to be more accurate in the 1936 election than that of the *Digest* or he would return the money to the newspapers that paid for the poll. The *Washington Post* trumpeted Gallup's challenge by renting a dirigible and flying it around Washington to advertise the launch of Gallup's column on October 20, 1935. Risking ruin, Gallup predicted a victory for Roosevelt. Gallup even had the effrontery to offer exact (and reasonably accurate) predictions of exactly how badly the *Literary Digest* would do in predicting the election.

The *Literary Digest,* with a rolling tabulation based on millions of postcards solicited from lists of automobile owners and telephone subscribers, predicted a landslide for Alf Landon and ridiculed the notion that a rival poll with a small sample size could predict anything. They made much of the fact that a Detroit newspaper had "not been able to find anyone who has ever been mailed a ballot . . . or who has been approached or asked an opinion" by this new rival organization. "On the other hand, we do find at least one in twenty, in all walks in life, who have received their LITERARY DIGEST ballots." Gallup's point, well known to statisticians at the time but not understood by the public, was that a scientific sample of a few thousand offers far more basis for confidence than does a self-selected sample of millions. The whole idea of random sampling had to be established in the public mind before challenges such as the *Literary Digest's* could be vanquished.[13]

As we know, Roosevelt won, the *Digest* went out of business, and Gallup's ambitions were realized: he achieved widespread acceptance for the notion that a relatively small scientific sample of public opinion could accurately reflect the views of the entire nation.

But Gallup's vision for the role of the opinion poll was even grander than predicting elections and clarifying mandates. He invoked the same ideal of face-to-face democracy we have emphasized throughout our story, in variations from Athenian democracy to the

American Founders and the debate over the Rhode Island referendum. Gallup argued that what was distinctive about the town meeting was that "the people gathered in one room to discuss and to vote on the questions of the community." As he explained: "There was a free exchange of opinions in the presence of all the members. The town meeting was a simple and effective way of articulating public opinion, and the decisions made by the meeting kept close to the public will."[14]

But as Gallup noted, this method was limited to the "small scale" for the same reasons given during the Rhode Island debate—the problem of gathering everyone together to hear the same arguments in preparation for a vote. Gallup, however, felt that with the combination of modern technology and the public opinion poll (or "sampling referendum" as he called it), this problem had finally been overcome. "The New England town meeting has, in a sense, been restored" he proclaimed. It has, in fact, been adapted for the whole nation:

> The wide distribution of daily newspapers reporting the views of statesmen on issues of the day, the almost universal ownership of radios which bring the whole nation within the hearing of any voice, and now the advent of the sampling referendum which provides a means of determining quickly the response of the public to debate on issues of the day, have in effect created a town meeting on a national scale.[15]

For Gallup, the point about the New England town meeting was that everyone could meet together, hear the arguments on either side, and then vote. With the mass media, everyone in the entire nation could now hear the arguments on either side, and the actual voting by all citizens would not be necessary to have the effect of a town meeting. With a scientific sample, the opinions held by everyone could be reported with comparable accuracy. As Gallup concluded a triumphant lecture at Princeton University two years after the 1936 election, "The nation is literally in one great room. The newspapers and the radio conduct the debate on national issues . . . just as the townsfolk did in person in the old town meeting. And finally, through the process of the sampling referendum, the people, having heard the debate on both sides of every issue, can express their will."[16]

The town meeting, he believed, had now been adapted to the entire nation. "This time the whole nation is within the doors." What Gallup did not take into account was that while everyone might, in a sense, be in one great room, the room had become so big that few people were paying much attention. A "room" of millions creates the conditions for rational ignorance. If I have one vote in a few hundred and I can participate in the debate in my local town meeting, then I have reason to pay attention and participate, for my individual vote and my individual voice may well make a difference. Democracy is humanized by the scale of face-to-face discussion. But if I have only one vote out of millions, I have little reason to become engaged in the debate. I am literally lost in the multitude. I have little reason to pay attention. My views have only a small chance of being solicited by Gallup's "sampling referendum" on the question at issue. Hence, those opinions are unlikely to make a difference to the outcome. A New England town meeting of many millions is no longer a New England town meeting. It is simply another occasion for individuals to feel lost in the politics of mass society.

OPINIONS AND PSEUDO-OPINIONS
IN THE ECHO CHAMBER

The survey research industry has exploded since the time of Gallup and the other pioneers. About 20 million interviews are conducted each year in the United States. In a 1986 study, 23 percent of respondents reported having been interviewed at least once in the past twelve months. Hence, "average citizens stand a more than fair chance of being interviewed several times during their life-times."[17] Just as in ancient Athens, where the lottery was used so frequently that each citizen had a good chance of occupying a position of responsibility at some point in his lifetime, each American citizen now has a good chance of being consulted on several occasions by opinion polls. The difference, however, is that the Athenian lottery put citizens in councils, juries, and legislative commissions, where they had to become immersed in the competing arguments *before* they were asked to make a decision. Telephone polls consult you in your living room, without warning or preparation, in order to find out your views—when you may well have had no reason to develop any opinions whatsoever on the subject being asked.

This point was demonstrated dramatically by a psychologist named Eugene Hartley in 1946. At around the same time that *Magic Town* was being made, Hartley conducted surveys of college students at various universities in the New York area concerning their attitudes toward various ethnic groups. Should members of a given ethnic group be permitted to enter the country? Should they be entitled to become citizens? Should they be allowed to seek employment? Should they be permitted to move into your neighborhood? Would you admit them as members of your family?

Hartley probed student attitudes concerning forty-nine ethnic groups including Germans, Italians, Poles, Russians, Wallonians, and Pireneans. However, the "Wallonians" and "Pireneans" were purely imaginary groups. Nevertheless, a large majority of the students surveyed expressed far more opposition to giving Wallonians or Pireneans U.S. citizenship or employment or allowing them to live in their neighborhoods than they showed for almost all the other ethnic groups.[18] Imagine if the results of such a survey were presented today and those results were picked up by the media. Another "factoid," a dubious or false bit of information that is widely believed because it has been widely disseminated by the media, would have been created. Clearly, Hartley's survey was not reporting a previously existing opinion about the merits of admitting Wallonians or Pireneans as opposed to other groups. It was reporting an "attitude" that was created on the spot by the very process of participating in the survey.

Nearly three decades later, researchers at the University of Cincinnati obtained similar results in telephone surveys of the Greater Cincinnati area. They solicited opinions of the "Public Affairs Act of 1975." About one-third of the adult population offered opinions, expressing either support or opposition, even though the act was entirely fictitious. When various filters were included, however, such as, "Have you been interested enough in this to favor one side or the other?"—which gave respondents a chance to confess their ignorance—the number offering an opinion dropped substantially, to between 5 and 10 percent in the various studies.[19]

Yet the problem is deeper than might seem from the effectiveness of questions designed to filter from the poll respondents who have no opinion. The political scientist Philip Converse coined the term *nonattitudes* for opinions created on the spot in response to survey questions. In a path-breaking series of analyses of a national panel study, in which the same respondents were asked the same questions from 1956 to 1960, Converse concluded that the variation in their responses was essentially random. Analyzing responses to such issues as "The government should leave things like electric power and housing for private businessmen to handle," he concluded that "large portions of an electorate do not have meaningful beliefs, even on issues that have formed the basis for intense political controversy among elites for a substantial period of time."[20]

It was especially striking that the respondents in these panel studies were given every opportunity to say they had no opinion. In the expectation that many people would have no opinions on or attitudes to some questions, Converse explains, "We had taken elaborate precautions to remove such people from any sense of obligation to respond":

> The battery of issue items was prefaced by a statement . . . that "different things are important to different people, so we don't expect everyone to have an opinion about all of these (things)." Furthermore, as each item in the battery was read, the respondent

was explicitly asked whether or not he had an opinion on the matter and only if he said that he did was he further asked what his opinion was.[21]

These efforts to filter out the people who had not thought about the question were successful enough that up to 35 percent of the sample confessed that they had no opinion on the questions Converse analyzed. But the findings of random variation over time "were computed for the subset of people who *did* lay claim to some opinion; the many no-opinion people were set aside" (emphasis added). When Converse put the no-opinion people together with the respondents whose opinions seemed to vary randomly over time, he was led to conclude that "something less than 20 per cent of the total sample fell into the category of real and stable attitudes on the items. The remaining 80 per cent represented confessions of 'no opinion' or statistically random responses." But most of these *seemed,* from observations at any one time, to have opinions. "It was a *minority* within this 80 per cent which took advantage of our invitation not to bother fabricating an opinion. When attitudes are asked for in such a setting, people are remarkably obliging."[22] As the political scientist Russell Neuman notes about these data: "Most respondents feel obliged to have an opinion, in effect, to help the interviewer out. . . . In effect, opinions are invented on the spot."[23]

Some have argued that the random variation in opinions over time may be the result of measurement error. A question may be ambiguous, for example, or not closely related to the "true opinion" that is being measured. In other words, while Converse argues that there really is no attitude there at all, some of his critics argue that there may actually be an attitude or an opinion but that we have difficulty measuring it. Either way, surveys reporting such results are not reporting what they *appear* to be presenting—the existence of an attitude or opinion that corresponds closely to what is being reported.

Undoubtedly, both explanations apply to some people under some conditions. The volatility in responses surveys obtain from many citizens is sometimes the result of there being no opinion to measure, and sometimes it is the result of ambiguities or misunderstandings about the questions. Furthermore, even when the respondent has an attitude or opinion to be measured, it may well be superficial. It may be little more than a vague impression stemming from headlines and sound bites or from brief conversations with friends who also may have thought little about the issue.

When the fleeting and volatile nature of many polls is combined with the mass media, nonexistent opinions may take on a life of their own. As the metaphor of the echo chamber suggests, television and polling reverberate together. Poll results are reported in the media and are bounced back by the public in further polls, regardless of whether the initial results had any substantial thought behind them.[24]

A RATIONAL PUBLIC?

When President Ford campaigned in San Antonio in 1976 (in the Texas primary against Ronald Reagan), he was offered Mexican food. With characteristic gusto, he bit into a hot tamale, neglecting to shuck it. The resulting picture of the president's discomfort made the evening news broadcasts and the *New York Times*. The political scientist and Clinton campaign adviser Samuel Popkin opens his book with this story, arguing that the unshucked tamale offers a "cue" Mexican-American voters should use to draw conclusions about President Ford and how much he knows about Mexican-Americans and their interests. Television viewers can pick up such cues about candidate positions without investing a lot of time and effort, as a by-product of other things they do. They can find important cues, for example, from watching the evening news. Cues may be based on limited information but they offer a shorthand from which voters can draw reasonable inferences.

There is undoubtedly some truth in Popkin's notion that viewers pick up cues from the mass media. Indeed, a number of experiments demonstrate that what citizens are interested in is subject to "priming" from whatever they have seen most recently on the evening news.[25] Yet whether a campaigner has difficulty biting into a tamale—and whether television happens to capture the event—is a slim basis for restoring the claims to rationality of the "reasoning voter," as Popkin aspires to do. In fact, it is arguable that any Mexican-American voter who paid attention to the campaign as a whole would probably have seen that Ford was positioning himself to appeal to Mexican-Americans far more than his challenger, Ronald Reagan.

At a time when Republican registration was still small in Texas, the primary contest was actually decided by about 280,000 Democratic crossover votes in Reagan's favor, mostly from supporters of George Wallace who were disappointed at the recent Democratic primary failures of their candidate in other states. Reagan launched an explicit, televised appeal to these voters on the basis that he could win the nomination of his party, while Wallace could not win the nomination of his. Reagan pounded Ford on conservative themes, particularly the issues of whether we were giving back the Panama Canal and whether Kissinger was sacrificing our policy in Africa in order to cultivate black voters in the United States. The Wallace voters to whom Reagan was appealing had little sympathy for minorities, whether blacks or Mexican-Americans. The unshucked tamale cue was largely irrelevant to the outcome, and, in fact, Mexican-American voters inclined to vote Republican would have had a more plausible supporter of their interests at the time in Ford than in Reagan(whose message was carefully crafted to appeal to extremely conservative crossover voters generally hostile to their interests).[26]

Hence, Mexican-American voters would have been seriously misled by the cue of the unshucked tamale. The production of cues comes from such an inevitably incomplete, manipulated, and accidental process of media and campaign coverage that it is hard to credit the prospects for rational analysis of the outputs when the inputs have such limitations. Later I shall explore whether there are ways to improve those inputs to public opinion by helping the public to create cues for itself in a less accidental and more rational manner. Deliberative polling, for example, is intended to facilitate the public's creating more rational cues for itself on national television.

The tenuousness of the information shortcuts citizens employ in evaluating cues in the media was dramatized by a recent *Washington Post* replication of the survey on the fictitious Public Affairs Act of 1975. In 1995, for the twentieth "un-anniversary" of the original nonexistent legislation, the *Post* commissioned a poll on whether the act should be repealed. But in addition to replicating the original study, the *Post* added two versions of a further question, to separate random samples, which mentioned either that President Clinton or that the Republican Congress advocated repeal of the act. The Clinton and Republican Congress cues had a dramatic effect on Democratic and Republican respondents. Knowing nothing about the Public Affairs Act of 1975 they could, nevertheless, determine whether they supported its repeal merely on the basis of whether Clinton or the Republican Congress had taken a position.[27]

Popkin's argument in support of cues is one of two major attempts to find a new basis for rationality for the American voter. Popkin's point is that, despite rational ignorance, voters can learn enough from cues like the unshucked tamale to draw a reasonable range of inferences about candidates. A second argument for construing voter behavior as rational is the claim that although *individual* citizens may hold superficial and ill-informed opinions, nonetheless, when all the opinions are *put together,* the collective public's opinion achieves a greater rationality. There may be a "rational public" even though individual opinions exhibit all the problems we have discussed. My stupidity and yours, my random volatility and yours, may, in fact, cancel each other out. The aggregate views of the society have far greater stability than individual views would suggest, since the variation from some in one direction is canceled out in the whole by the variation by others in the opposite direction.

Political scientists Benjamin Page and Robert Y. Shapiro offer an incisive and original case for this position. They argue that while individual citizens may know little about an issue, and while their individual opinions may fluctuate wildly, when we take the whole society together, a different kind of public opinion is revealed. Collectively, public opinion can end up being more rational and stable than anyone might suppose from examining the fluctuations of individual opinions. They introduce this notion with the example of a single imaginary citizen's views on a subject greatly debated in Congress in the early 1980s—whether we should build the MX missile and, if so, how many.[28]

Imagine a single individual questioned many times about this issue. The responses about how many missiles should be built might range, Page and Shapiro imagine, from zero to forty, but when averaged the number would likely be something in between, say, twenty or twenty-five. Page and Shapiro propose that we take this average as "a fairly reliable estimate of the individual's long-term preference" for the number of missiles to be produced.

Similarly, we can average hundreds of responses in a survey and take that as a representation of the collective average view. Random fluctuations in individual views will tend to cancel each other out. Indeed, Page and Shapiro show that for the same questions in which Converse had found random individual fluctuations—questions like the role of government and business in producing electric power and housing—there had been relatively stable collective preferences: the number of individuals favoring each option remained reasonably stable over time. While there was a great deal of random fluctuation in individual opinions, these tended to cancel each other out. Movements of some people in one direction were balanced by movements of others in the opposite direction.

It is worth asking, however: What is an individual's "long-term opinion," as constructed from averaging many responses? Or what is a "collective opinion" that is a statistical construct of many responses, many of which vary wildly, and that is constructed from many individual impressions of bits of arguments and scraps of information?

Consider the MX case. How "rational" can we consider a collective preference to build, say, twenty-five missiles, when the public has so little information about, or engagement with, the issue? While the MX missile debate was raging, a Carnegie Commission used it as a defining example of our lack of civic literacy. "Citizens have tried with . . . bafflement to follow the debate over the MX missile, with its highly technical jargon of deterrence and counter-deterrence." The authors warned: "Unless we find better ways to educate ourselves as citizens, we run the risk of drifting unwittingly into a new kind of Dark Age— a time when small cadres of specialists will control knowledge and thus control the decision-making process."[29]

Can the simple expedient of statistically averaging responses by hundreds or thousands of ordinary citizens, nearly all of whom are uninitiated into these complexities, really represent the kind of "rational" opinion that democratic theory would ask us to expect of citizens?

More specifically, the MX debate involved complex issues of strategic doctrine. Were our Midgetman missiles vulnerable to a Soviet first strike? If we built the MX were we destabilizing the world by *introducing* the possibility that we could hit the Soviets with a first strike? Would it be better to develop the MX but not deploy it so that we could *threaten* the Soviets without giving them an incentive to step up their own missile production as a defense against our new first-strike threat? Should we develop it as a bargaining chip in arms-control talks? The antiballistic missile system (ABM) worked as a bargaining chip, but other weapons systems (the cruise missile, for one) that were supposedly developed as bargaining chips took on a life of their own and could never be canceled. Which would be the likely fate of the MX missile if it were developed under the "bargaining chip" rationale? The fate of the ABM or that of the cruise missile?

It would be absurd to think that any significant proportion of the American public developed a sophisticated grasp of *any* of these questions. Yet these were the main items in the elite debate at the time. Furthermore, emphasizing one factor over another could lead to the conclusion that no missiles whatsoever should be built because they destabilized world peace with the threat of a nuclear first strike, or that we should build as many as possible, to counter the possibility of a Russian first strike, or that we should develop the missile but not build it. The rational conclusion swings wildly between extremes, from none to many to development without deployment. To take a specific number of missiles as a long-term average and claim this number as a representation of "long-term preference" on the part of citizens who were not even aware of the arguments is to draw inferences that would probably surprise all the citizens to whom these preferences were being attributed. It seems more accurate to say that on this issue, the public was *not* rational. It was not thoughtful or self-conscious in its attempts to weigh the competing arguments and come to some conclusion. Rather, it was only dimly aware of some of the complex arguments, and while its impressions could be quantified, they fell so short of democratic expectations as to be lamentable.

Just for purposes of contrast, imagine what might have happened if the inertia of rational ignorance had somehow been transcended and the mass public had become knowledgeable about the MX missile debate. Perhaps they would have decided to abandon the project because of the destabilizing effects of introducing a first-strike capability. Or perhaps they would have concluded that we needed to develop the missile as a bargaining chip or that we needed to rush into production to respond to the Soviet threat. Any of these options reached after widespread knowledge of the arguments and a collective engagement with the debate might have brought us a public opinion worth having. What the polls reported instead was a statistical aggregation of vague impressions formed mostly in ignorance of sharply competing arguments—any one of which, if accepted, would lead to an entirely different conclusion.

THE AMERICAN PROCESS:
A MACHINE THAT TRANSFORMS ITSELF

The American Constitution has often been compared to a machine—in a well-known phrase, "a machine that would go of itself."[30] But in our era we have machines unlike any known to the American Founders, machines that bear the comparison even more suggestively: thinking machines.

There are two main approaches to using computers as thinking machines. Traditional "A.I.," or artificial intelligence, would have us completely specify a problem and then construct a list of rules for the computer's "thought processes" to follow in dealing with that problem. A second approach, often identified with "neural networks," attempts to mimic the human brain by creating programs that adapt to what they are exposed to. In this approach, the machine attempts to follow the path of human learning. A thinking machine that learns develops in unexpected ways and can, it seems, eventually surpass the results of traditional A.I.

The American Founders, in creating the Constitution, set in motion a collective mechanism comparable to this second kind of thinking machine—a machine that has been learning and transforming itself since its creation. The actions of such a machine cannot be captured by reconstructing the rules of the designers or founders. The operative rules keep changing as the machine develops, or "learns." By contrast, a machine constructed on the first model—unchanging rules determined in full by its creators—could best be understood by what Constitutional lawyers call "originalism"—following the full list of rules fashioned by its creators as they intended them. But for a thinking machine that learns, those rules and intentions would have less relevance. They would help, but they would tell only the beginning of the story.

To understand such a machine we require a continuing dynamic assessment of growth, of the system's learning, most of which has occurred since its beginnings. Such a machine would probably change in ways that would surprise the original designers. And our machine is like that. Would not the Founders of the original American Constitutional design be surprised to find out what happened to the Electoral College and the election of senators and to discover the role of television, the rise of mass democracy (through primaries as well as referendums in many states), the development of political parties, the rise of opinion polling, and, perhaps most of all, the enormous scale of the national state and its federal government?

This collective artificial life form, the living machine of our American system, has already had an extraordinary life by international standards. We have by far the world's oldest written constitution, although some argue that since so many of our conventions and understandings are not part of the text we are not so different from Britain and Israel, which have constitutional traditions without a written constitution.[31]

Whether these norms and informal understandings are thought of as part of the American Constitution, they are a key mechanism for change. The system can be transformed in dramatic ways even if there are few if any formal changes in the law or in the Constitution. Sometimes the transformation depends on a change in the commonly accepted notion of a role—like that of presidential elector or of delegate to a national party convention—sometimes it comes from a new mode of communication (the mass newspaper, radio, or television), or sometimes it is fueled by a new method of assessing public attitudes, such as opinion polling.

Sometimes, however, the Constitution itself changes. It is not merely a matter of norms or roles or expectations but rather an official change through passage of a Constitutional amendment. But as we saw in the case of the Seventeenth Amendment, the informal changes can make the official change virtually an established fact by the time it actually occurs. The people acquired the effective power to select U.S. senators long before the Constitution was modified to reflect this transformation. Furthermore, when the Constitution does change, it may do so in ways that are far more informal than the official amendment process would suggest. All the factors we have mentioned, particularly public opinion and the way key actors conceptualize their roles, may lead to dramatic changes, even when few Constitutional amendments have been passed. There may, for example, be an overwhelming change in collective understanding, a change in the moral premises of the political culture, which turns out to be far more important than the text of any Constitutional amendment. Some interpreters of the U.S. Constitution have argued that many of its biggest changes can be understood not as amendments but rather as transformations in collective understanding that permanently alter the way the Constitution is interpreted by the courts and by legislators. The transformation in our collective understanding of the role of government in the national economy after the New Deal, for example, cannot be captured by amendments. But it rendered the laws of the previous period, termed the "Lochner" era by lawyers (a period when the Court struck down attempts by government to regulate market transactions), as irrelevant as they would have been had they been amended out of existence.

Artificial intelligence will reduce the thinking processes of a machine to a series of rules of inference. With neural networks, those rules cannot all be specified in advance. They develop over time as the system adapts to its inputs. With the Constitutional "machine" we can think of various rules or principles, some of which were adopted at the framing, some of which developed in later periods.[32] These rules or principles are key not only to understanding the system's operation but also to understanding its legitimacy. The Constitution is a system of accepted rules and principles. To the degree those rules and principles retain public loyalty and acceptance, the system maintains its legitimacy. Even when the details of the principles are not widely understood, the fact that they have acceptance, the fact that they will be supported when questioned, is an important part of what keeps the system in place.

The American Founders knew that they were creating a government that would rest on public opinion. As the historian Gordon Wood observes: "No government, Americans told themselves over and over, had ever before so completely set its roots in the sentiments and aims of its citizens." All power was "derived from public opinion."[33] This is the point of all the popular rhetoric about the "consent of the governed."

But how is public opinion to be consulted so that it can be brought to bear on *Constitutional* issues? Who speaks for the people when the issue is how to renew or change the Constitution? There is one simple answer many commentators and citizens offer to such a question. There is no need to consult public opinion directly or informally. We have legal procedures in place, specified by the law operative at any specific time, and those *procedures* tell us how the Constitution can be changed.

The American system would never have been born, however, if that were the whole answer. And after its beginnings, many of its major changes cannot be captured by a mere focus on procedures. In fact, some of the most important changes are difficult to understand by such a focus. Article V of the Constitution specifies the ways in which the Constitution can be amended. But many of the most dramatic changes in the Constitution either violate, or make no significant use of, Article V.

Begin with the beginning. Viewed in terms of the law at the time, the Constitution was illegal at its birth. There was an existing system of national government, the Articles of Confederation, that provided no basis for such a Constitutional Convention. As Gouverneur Morris noted during the debates in Philadelphia, "This Convention is unknown to the Confederation."

The Congress (as constituted by the Articles of Confederation) had initially ignored the proposed Constitutional Convention. After a majority of states elected delegates, however, Congress issued a call for the convention, "for the sole and express purpose of revising the Articles of Confederation and reporting to Congress and the several legislatures" the proposed changes that would render "the federal constitution adequate to the exigencies of Government and the preservation of the Union."

The plan the Founders devised at Philadelphia went beyond this mandate. The new document could not be considered a mere amendment to the Articles of Confederation. It was, in fact, an entirely new constitution. The plan was not submitted to the state legislatures, as the Articles and the Congress required. It was sent, instead, to elected conventions, separate from the legislatures, in the various states. Furthermore, it was to come into effect when nine of the states ratified it. By contrast, the Articles of Confederation required unanimous approval of the thirteen state legislatures for any changes.

Madison argued at the Constitutional Convention that ratification by convention should be the required mode of approval. Not only would the state legislatures be less inclined to approve the new system, but the state convention was taken as a method for gaining approval from the people themselves. A treaty could be founded on the legislatures; a constitution, Madison argued, must be "founded on the people."[34] "The people were in fact, the fountain of all power, and by resorting to them, all difficulties were got over. They could alter constitutions as they pleased."[35]

As we saw in the debate over Rhode Island's referendum, the Founders envisaged state conventions as a method of consulting the people. A referendum, which would have consulted the people even more directly, was not something they contemplated. It would have raised all the issues of direct democracy (a "democracy" rather than an extended republic) that they were so concerned to avoid.

The real source of legitimacy was the people. The Articles of Confederation, after all, had not been ratified by the people directly, but only by the state legislatures. The Founders thought that they had come up with a distinctive innovation for consulting the people—the Constitutional Convention. The convention, of course, is the embodiment of our ideal of face-to-face democracy. It was also an innovation. "It was an extraordinary invention, the most distinctive institutional contribution," Wood notes, "the American Revolutionaries made to Western politics." It provided for a basis for political authority separate from the legislature and thus could be used to limit what legislatures did.[36]

The idea of the convention went back in English history to any gathering of the nation outside of Parliament. Initially, it was seen as a kind of defective Parliament. But whatever its defects, it also provided a precedent for revolutionary change to protect the rights of Englishmen. The Americans could cite the fact that William and Mary were given the British throne in the Glorious Revolution of 1688 by a body that called itself a "convention." The colonists had become familiar with many gatherings that sprang up during the Stamp Act crisis and the later events leading up to the American Revolution. These conventions and congresses purported to speak for the people to present their grievances. The irregularity or informality of the convention was part of its power. Its separateness from established authority gave it the independence necessary for it to speak for the people, even if many of its members might well overlap with the legislature at the time.

Madison argued in *Federalist* no. 40 for the legitimacy of the Constitutional Convention despite its irregularity. An informal method of consulting the people was necessary, since the people could not all be gathered together. It was by such methods that the states brought about their revolution against the British, and it was by such methods that they arrived at many of their individual constitutions. All of these factors require "some *informal and unauthorized propositions,* made by some patriotic and respectable citizens or number of citizens," Madison argued.

Even if the American founding required an irregular method, a Constitutional Convention that went beyond the law at the time, it might still be argued that the American system, once in place, undergoes Constitutional change only when the Constitution is officially amended according to the procedures laid down in Article V.

But the amendment that has probably done more than any other to change the character of the American system, the Fourteenth Amendment, did not satisfy the procedural niceties set out in Article V. The eleven Southern states were excluded from the Congress that approved it. As one Northern legislator noted at the time: "The Southern States are competent, at least, to contribute a portion of the three-fourths required . . . for the purpose of ratifying amendments, but [are] out of the Union for the purpose of aiding in proposing amendments."[37] One constitutional theorist, Bruce Ackerman, has tried to explain the eventual legitimacy of the Fourteenth Amendment by suggesting that the "Thirty-Ninth Congress [which approved the Amendment] may best be viewed as a Constitutional Convention."[38] Like the original convention, the Congress voting on the Fourteenth Amendment was a gathering of the people that did not satisfy the procedural niceties of the time, but because it distilled the mobilized deliberation of the nation, it came to be accepted and it acquired legitimacy.

Ackerman's argument is that sometimes there are Constitutional Moments when the people are seriously engaged and deliberate. As we have seen, he counts three such moments in American history thus far—the Revolution, Reconstruction, and the New Deal.[39] Most of the time, however, we live in a period of "normal politics," when the masses are disengaged, and few of our criteria are satisfied. Instead of the participation, deliberation, and political equality that comes from a Constitutional Moment, normal politics features mass withdrawal by the people and an interest-group politics dominated by elites. On Ackerman's view, the people rarely speak. But they can be given greater voice, even when the occasion lacks the authority of a constitutional convention.

4

WHO ARE THE PEOPLE?

WHOSE DECLARATION OF INDEPENDENCE?

America was forged in the name of general principles justifying institutions that practiced particular exclusions. As the exclusions were dropped, one by one, "the people" became more numerous and more diverse. Representation and public opinion had to change as our conception of the relevant public became more inclusive.

In colonial times, the right to vote was generally limited by property qualifications. Not all white males, but only propertied white males, were permitted to vote. English notions of suffrage, inherited by the American colonies, were based on "the belief, as old as the emergence of the House of Commons itself, that so long as the landowners directly paid the bulk of public taxes it was not inequitable or unjust to confine Commons elections to them." This belief was embodied in the "forty shillings" law of 1430, which mandated that in order to vote a man had to own land or its equivalent capable of yielding forty shillings in income a year.[1]

The "true reason of requiring any qualifications with regard to property in voters," wrote William Blackstone in his eighteenth-century legal commentary on the laws of England, "is to exclude such persons as are in so mean a situation as to be esteemed to have no will of their own."[2] The concern was that those without property could easily be coerced into voting for whomever they were told.

One hundred years later, Anthony Trollope could convincingly portray exactly this phenomenon in England in his novel *Phineas Finn,* a perceptive portrait of nineteenth-century British politics. Phineas has made a political career arguing for suffrage reform and greater democracy. The reforms he advocates complicate his career because, at various points, his constituencies are reformed out of existence. He is put up as the candidate for Loughton, a rotten borough controlled by the earl of Brentford. On his first visit to the borough:

> Each individual man of Loughton then present took an opportunity during the meeting of whispering into Mr. Finn's ear a word or two to show that he also was admitted to the secret councils of the borough,—that he too could see the inside of the arrangement. "Of course we must support the Earl," one said. "Never mind what you hear about a Tory candidate, Mr. Finn," whispered a second; "the Earl can do what he pleases here." And it seemed to Phineas that it was thought by them all to be rather a fine thing to be thus held in the hand by an English nobleman. Phineas could not but reflect upon this as he lay in his bed at the Loughton inn. The great political question on which the political world was engrossed up in London was the enfranchisement of Englishmen,—of Englishmen down to the rank of artisans and labourers;—and yet when he found himself in contact with individual Englishmen, with men even very much above the artisan and the labourer, he found that they rather liked being bound hand and foot, and being kept as tools in the political pocket of a rich man. Every one of those Loughton tradesmen was proud of his own personal subjection to the Earl![3]

As the earl himself explains to Phineas later, in reply to the comment that "they all seemed to be very obliging": "Yes they are. There isn't a house in the town, you know, let for longer than seven years, and most of them merely from year to year. And, do you know, I haven't a farmer on the property with a lease,—not one; and they don't want leases. They know they're safe. But I do like the people round me to be of the same way of thinking as myself about politics."[4]

By the time of Trollope's writing, the property qualifications inherited by the Americans from the English had largely been reformed out of existence. But waves of immigrants were still to come, and the political machines of the cities employed many of the same processes to garner the votes of the poor. Extending the vote to the poor and vulnerable gives them a voice. But creating a degree of economic independence allows the vote to be more independent and meaningful. The vote is only one dimension of inclusion, but it is of great symbolic and strategic importance.

Between the American Revolution and the Constitutional Convention, no state passed laws democratizing the property qualification for voting. The Founders left the matter of suffrage qualifications to each state. But many of the Founders clearly envisaged the great mass of the people voting, at least for the one explicitly democratic branch, the House of Representatives. Madison, for example, in *Federalist* no. 57 asked, "Who are the electors of the federal representatives? Not the rich, more than the poor; not the learned, more than the ignorant; not the haughty heirs of distinguished names, more than the humble sons of obscure and unpropitious fortune. The electors are to be the great body of the people of the United States." And some states allowed all adult males to vote for the representatives to their ratifying conventions for the Constitution, even though they retained property qualifications for other elections in their state constitutions.

Depreciation of the value of paper money broadened the franchise over time in some states. Such reform by inflation began to be supplemented by an explicit moral argument on the basis that those who fought for freedom should be entitled to vote. "Who stood in the ranks as soldiers and fought the battles of the Revolutionary War?" asked one local newspaper (the *Fredericktown Hornet*). "Is not the poor man now bound to do military duty? And do not the farmers and mechanics now fill the ranks of the militia companies? The soldier is as much entitled to vote as the Captain of the company or the Colonel of the regiment."[5]

Thomas Jefferson had, in fact, proposed adult manhood suffrage for the territories as early as his draft of the Northwest Ordinance in 1784.[6] And it was later, in the heyday of Jeffersonian democracy, that most states managed to achieve the reform.

But the author of the Declaration of Independence inspired far broader expansions of the suffrage than its extension to poor white males. The dramatic declaration that gave birth to the American Republic—"We hold these truths to be self-evident: that all men are created equal, that they are endowed by their Creator with certain unalienable rights, that among these are life, liberty and the pursuit of happiness"—has inspired claims to equal rights on the part of men who, because of their race, were not citizens and on the part of citizens, who, because of their gender, were not men.

Although Jefferson owned perhaps two hundred slaves at the time he drafted the Declaration, and he owned about that number when he died, he had, in numerous ways, expressed his opposition to slavery.[7] Jefferson's draft of the Declaration included a long condemnation of George III for his support of the slave trade. "He has waged cruel war against human nature itself, violating its most sacred rights of life and liberty in the persons of a distant people who never offended him, captivating and carrying them into slavery in another hemisphere." Here is a recognition, on Jefferson's part, that the slave trade violated the "most sacred rights of life and liberty." And, Jefferson continued, the king was "determined to keep open a market where Men should be bought and sold."[8] In his draft of the Declaration, Jefferson applied the term *men* to slaves at the same time he affirmed that all men are created equal, and he asserted that the natural rights that provided the basis for the Declaration also applied to slaves.

Jefferson later noted that these passages were "struck out in complaisance to South Carolina and Georgia, who had never attempted to restrain the importation of slaves and who, on the contrary, still

wished to continue it." He also felt little support from the North—
"Though their people have very few slaves themselves, yet they had
been pretty considerable carriers of them to others."[9] Hence a good
case can be made that Jefferson's own draft of the Declaration included the condemnation of slavery and included an explicit basis for
a logic of inclusion—a logic that would include blacks as well as
whites as holders of rights to life and liberty.

In his *Notes on the State of Virginia,* however, Jefferson offered
some notorious observations on the capacities of blacks, observations
typical of the views of his time but dispiriting to those of us who
would picture Jefferson as a prime advocate of universal liberty.
"Comparing them by their faculties of memory, reason and imagination," Jefferson said, "it appears to me, that in memory they are equal
to the whites, in reason much inferior, as I think one could scarcely be
found capable of tracing the investigations of Euclid, and that in imagination they are dull tasteless and anomalous."[10]

Whatever his views of the capacities of blacks, Jefferson had a
long history of advocating their rights. As a young lawyer, for example, Jefferson attempted to argue that the grandson of a mulatto was
not subject to servitude because on the grounds of "the law of nature"
we "are all born free." He lost his case.[11] He later said, in his *Notes on
the State of Virginia,* that because of slavery, "I tremble for my country when I reflect that God is just" and that "His justice cannot sleep
forever."[12]

ALL MEN? FROM DOUGLASS
TO LINCOLN VERSUS DOUGLAS

In the 1840s, a former piece of property, the one-time slave who
named himself Frederick Douglass, began to emerge as the great
spokesman for extending the ideals of the Declaration of Independence to the enslaved blacks. In one of many speeches on the subject,
Douglass noted in 1858 that "the American Republic" had been

launched only eighty-two years earlier and that the "great act which gave it being was the Declaration of Independence." And that Declaration was based on the central principle that "all men are entitled to life, liberty and to an equal chance for happiness." The Founders told a "then listening world" that "they would establish a Government which should secure these cardinal rights to the weakest and humblest of the American people."[13]

After noting that this solemn pledge was made before God, as well as before mankind, Douglass avers that "I do not doubt that it was the purpose of your fathers to form just such a government as the Declaration of Independence shadows forth as the true one." Note that he says "your fathers," not his. Born of a slave mother, whom he scarcely knew, and an unknown or at least unacknowledged white father, he does not recognize any descent from the Founding Fathers of white America. But his patriotic affirmation is for the form of government that the Declaration "shadows forth." The true government is the one that would realize the principles of the Declaration more universally, the one that would include people like Douglass.

He does not doubt the sincerity of the American Founders. "They really believed in liberty, they believed in humanity, they believed in human progress and in human elevation." He applauds the fact that they "stated their principles in the broadest and most comprehensive terms they could command." Because they regarded slavery as "a transient, not a permanent, feature of American society, they made no provision for the hateful thing in the Constitution." The rhetoric of American principles is " 'we the people,' never we, the white people. Neither in the Constitution nor in the Declaration of Independence, is there a single reference to the subject of color."[14]

In the same speech, "The Reproach and Shame of the American Government" (delivered August 2, 1858), he rebukes some recent Fourth of July speeches he has heard. The Fourth of July, marking the original Declaration of Independence "is still celebrated, but not as a festival of Liberty. With many it is the great day selected for the assassination of Liberty." He rebukes the July 4 speech that "leaves unsaid the only word which is in keeping with the great principles and purposes of the Declaration of Independence." A speech that fails to mention slavery is just like the speech of "any old Tory" in 1776. "As they would have had your fathers seal their lips on the subject of British oppression for the safety of the union with England," modern speakers "would have us seal our lips on the subject of American Slavery for the sake of the Union with the South."[15] The American founding was a revolt against tyranny and against the deprivation of rights. A celebration of the principles of that Revolution, as Douglass claims they would be interpreted by any of the Founders, would demand speaking out against slavery. The country would never have been founded had the original American patriots acquiesced to injustice.

Douglass had already given his own speech for the July 4 holiday. In one version, delivered on July 5, 1852, he asked, "What to the Slave is the Fourth of July?" He confronts the astonishingly simple logic that if all men are created equal and endowed with inalienable rights, and if Negroes are men, then they must also be endowed with rights. To secure the inference, all he needs argue is that Negroes are men. He needs "to affirm the equal manhood of the negro race" even though to do so seems beyond dispute:

> Is it not astonishing that, while we are plowing, planting and reaping, using all kinds of mechanical tools, erecting houses, constructing bridges, building ships, working in metals of brass, iron, copper, silver and gold; that while we are reading, writing, and cyphering, acting as clerks, merchants, and secretaries, having among us lawyers, doctors, ministers, poets, authors, editors, orators and teachers; that while we are engaged in all manner of enterprises common to other men—digging gold in California, capturing the whale in the Pacific, feeding sheep and cattle on the hillside, living moving, acting, thinking, planning, living in families as husbands, wives and children, and, above all, confessing

and worshiping the christian's God, and looking hopefully for life and immortality beyond the grave,—we are called upon to prove that we are men![16]

Douglass establishes that Negroes are "men." He sees it granted by American principles that "men" are "entitled to liberty." The argument is part of the Declaration of Independence. Must he debate that slavery is wrong, that it is a violation of the rights of liberty? How is such a question to be settled? "Is it to be settled by the rules of logic and argumentation?" The answer is so obvious that to debate it seriously would be "to make myself ridiculous, and to offer an insult to your understanding." He will not waste his time seriously debating it:

> What! am I to argue that it is wrong to make men brutes, to rob them of their liberty, to work them without wages, to keep them ignorant of their relations to their fellow men, to beat them with sticks, to flay their flesh with the lash, to load their limbs with irons, to hunt them with dogs. . . . Must I argue that a system, thus stained with blood and stained with pollution, is wrong? No; I will not. I have better employment for my time and strength than such arguments would imply.[17]

But while the issues seemed beyond argument to Douglass and to many of his listeners, the same issues defined the core of one of the most elaborate public debates ever staged in the United States: the debates, tied to the 1858 U.S. Senate race in Illinois, between Stephen A. Douglas and Abraham Lincoln. Frederick Douglass knew full well the stakes in the Lincoln-Douglas debates. In his 1858 speech "The Reproach and Shame of the American Government," he commented on the unfolding spectacle, one that had captured the national imagination via newspaper reports. "The truth is," he noted, "that Slavery and Anti-Slavery is at the bottom of the contest."[18]

The Lincoln-Douglas debates were a major step in the democratization of Senate elections. It was a bold departure to have slates of state legislators publicly pledged to support one candidate or the other (since it was the legislature, rather than the people directly, that ultimately made the choice of Senator). But it was an even bolder departure to have a series of face-to-face debates on issues of principle, with large audiences, whose size was limited only by the power of the human voice, and with the rest of the country as witness via newspaper reports. As one historian notes, "The campaign was the first to be reported in modern fashion. In two ways, it made journalistic history. For the first time correspondents traveled with candidates, and for the first time a series of political speeches was reported stenographically."[19]

Frederick Douglass observed that his near-namesake "has a desperate case on his hands. . . . He has to defend the Dred Scott decision in one breath, and popular sovereignty in the next." Popular sovereignty required that a territory be able to decide for itself whether to allow slavery, but the Dred Scott decision "denies the right of a Territory to exclude slavery at all." After offering a lengthy analysis of Senator Douglas's opportunism, Douglass concludes that the senator is "one of the most restless, ambitious, boldest and most unscrupulous enemies with whom the cause of the colored man has to contend." The former slave observed: "It seems to me that the white Douglas should occasionally meet his deserts at the hands of a black one. Once I thought he was about to make the name respectable, but now I despair of him and must do the best I can for it myself."[20]

The interpretation of the Declaration of Independence was central to the Lincoln-Douglas debates. Lincoln said later, after being elected president, "I have never had a feeling politically that did not spring from the sentiments embodied in the Declaration of Independence." It seemed to provide an answer to a deep problem: "I have often pondered over the toils that were endured by the officers and soldiers of the army, who achieved that Independence. I have often inquired of myself what great principle or idea it was that kept this Confederacy so long together."[21] In the debates with Douglas, the Declaration framed the issue of principle: To whom did the rights enunciated in the

Declaration apply? And the debates were, like the Declaration before them, a public appeal to the common moral sense of mankind.

Lincoln set the tone with his "House Divided" speech of June 16, 1858. This was the opening of the campaign and preceded the seven debates, defining a position that was discussed extensively throughout the proceedings. It was also quoted at length by Frederick Douglass:

"A house divided against itself cannot stand." I believe this Government cannot endure permanently half Slave and half Free. . . . I do not expect the house to fall—but I do expect it will cease to be divided. It will become all one thing, or all the other. Either the opponents of Slavery will arrest the further spread of it, and place it where the public mind shall rest in the belief that it is in the course of ultimate extinction; or his advocates will push it forward till it shall become alike lawful in all the States—old as well as new, North as well as South. (2)[22]

Throughout the debates, Lincoln used the principles of the Declaration of Independence to argue that the rights defined in the Declaration ruled out slavery. The "House Divided" speech defined a forced choice: the country would have to move either one way or the other. The Declaration provided the basis for moving in the direction of freedom rather than slavery. It provided ground upon which Lincoln could stand, an Archimedean point, if you will, from which he could move the country in the desired direction, or at least upon which he could stand to arrest the spread of slavery. If the Declaration did not apply to blacks, then what other exceptions might be found? "I should like to know if taking this old Declaration of Independence, which declares that all men are equal upon principle and making exceptions to it where will it stop. If one man says it does not mean a negro, why not another say it does not mean some other man? If that Declaration is not the truth, let us get the statute book, in which we find it and tear it out!" (41).

Lincoln also appealed to patriotic sensibilities. The Declaration of

Independence was a declaration of freedom from the despotism of a king. But the arguments offered for denying rights to slaves were, in Lincoln's view, essentially the same arguments kings had always used to deny rights to their subjects. "Those arguments that are made, that the inferior race are to be treated with as much allowance as they are capable of enjoying," are the arguments "that kings have made for enslaving the people in all ages of the world." According to Lincoln, "All the arguments in favor of king-craft were of this class; they always bestrode the necks of the people, not that they wanted to do it, but because the people were better off for being ridden" (41).

Stephen Douglas soon answered that "Mr. Lincoln . . . reads from the Declaration of Independence that all men were created equal, and then asks how can you deprive a negro of that equality which God and the Declaration of Independence awards to him." Douglas replies by playing to the prejudice of his audience: "I do not regard the negro as my equal and positively deny that he is my brother or any kin to me whatsoever" (111).

Although we may today be surprised at hearing such racist opinions voiced so openly, these comments were, as a concession to proslavery opinion, particularly in the South, "the minimum . . . needed to maintain the Democratic party as a national party and to preserve popular government in a nation increasingly rent by a deep moral cleavage." Harry Jaffa observes that such a position may well have appeared to Douglas as "the choice of a lesser evil."[23] It is also worth noting, for our issue of inclusion, that Douglas repeatedly condemned the Know-Nothing Party, a powerful political force that campaigned against the rights of non–Anglo-Saxons and immigrants. Lincoln was publicly silent about the Know-Nothings, although he condemned them in private.

Douglas's main line of argument was to defend state sovereignty. Illinois had decided that free Negroes could not vote while "Maine, on the other hand, has said that they shall vote. Maine is a sovereign state, and has the power to regulate the qualifications of voters within her limits. I would never consent to confer the right of voting and of citizenship upon a negro, but still I am not going to quarrel with Maine for differing from me in opinion." Only by respecting state sovereignty has America prospered. "If we only adhere to that principle, we can go forward increasing in territory, in power, in strength and in glory until the Republic of America shall be the North Star that shall guide the friends of freedom throughout the civilized world" (113–114). *North Star* was the name of Frederick Douglass's anti-slavery paper. We can only speculate about his reaction to the other Douglas using the same image for an America that achieves freedom under state sovereignty for everyone *but* the slaves, and in the name of civilized freedom, as an inspiration for the world to follow.

But Douglas's most detailed reply to Lincoln's use of the Declaration was to point out that the Founders were slaveholders themselves; if they had meant to include blacks as bearers of the rights referred to in the Declaration, they would all have been hypocrites. "When Thomas Jefferson wrote that document he was the owner . . . of a large number of slaves. Did he intend to say in that Declaration that his negro slaves, which he held and treated as property, were created his equals by Divine law, and that he was violating the law of God every day of his life by holding them as slaves?" Douglas also points out that all the signers who owned slaves continued to do so and that at the time of the signing all thirteen colonies permitted slavery, which meant that every signer had a slaveholding constituency. "When you say that the Declaration of Independence includes the negro," Douglas concludes, "you charge the signers of it with hypocrisy" (294).

Lincoln replied with astonishment that Douglas could really be denying that the Founders meant the Declaration to apply to blacks. "I believe that the entire records of the world, from the date of the Declaration of Independence up to within three years ago, may be searched in vain for one single affirmation, from one single man, that the negro was not included in the Declaration of Independence." He doubts that Judge Douglas himself ever said so, or "that Washington ever said so, that any President ever said so, that any member of Congress ever said so, until the necessities of the present Democratic party, in regard to slavery, had to invent that affirmation" (298).

Lincoln also pointed out that Jefferson "trembled for his country when he remembered that God is just"—that is, when he thought of slavery. Later, Lincoln explained that in referring to slavery the Founders used "covert" language. Hoping that slavery would eventually disappear, they preferred that "there should be nothing on the great charter of liberty [the Constitution] suggesting that such a thing as negro slavery had ever existed among us. This is part of the evidence that the founders expected and intended the institution of slavery to come to an end" (385).

In the hindsight of modern discussions, Lincoln's position hardly seems radical. In fact, he went to pains to deny Douglas's charge that he was an advocate of "perfect social and political equality with the negro." Douglas, Lincoln responded, was playing with words, as if he were proving "a horse chestnut to be a chestnut horse." Lincoln saw differences between the races. Nevertheless, he defended the application to blacks of the rights defined in the Declaration. "There is no reason in the world why the negro is not entitled to all the rights enumerated in the Declaration of Independence, the right to life, liberty and the pursuit of happiness." What Lincoln wished, especially, to affirm was that "in the right to eat the bread, without leave of anybody else, which his own hand earns," the black man is "my equal and the equal of Judge Douglas, and the equal of every living man" (117).

In its time, even this position was radical. We can see this from the fact that even by the time of the Republican Nominating Convention of 1860—the convention of a party organized around its opposition to slavery—an amendment incorporating the principles of the Declaration of Independence was initially voted down. When the amendment was eventually included, it was accepted only on the basis that it had no "application in terms of racial equality."[24]

The debates themselves produced a mixed outcome. Douglas, of course, won reelection, but Lincoln won in terms of popular vote—125,430 to 121,609.[25] The cumbersome system of voting for state legislators pledged to one candidate or another translated the popular judgment of Senate candidates imperfectly. But the election remained an example of how Senate elections could be democratized, and they launched Lincoln onto the national stage, laying the moral groundwork for his presidency and, eventually, for the Emancipation Proclamation.

FROM PAPER RIGHTS TO VOTING RIGHTS

The Declaration of Independence defines a benchmark by which the rights of Americans can be judged. Progress for blacks, at least on paper, in realizing their rights under the Declaration came about through the Thirteenth Amendment to the Constitution, which granted them legal freedom; the Fourteenth Amendment, which granted them citizenship and equal protection of the laws; and the Fifteenth Amendment, which granted them the vote. But the power of the amendments was largely nullified in practice after the retreat from Reconstruction, most notably after the Hayes-Tilden Compromise of 1877.

The Republican Rutherford B. Hayes claimed victory in the 1876 presidential election by one electoral vote, but his victory relied on disputed electoral returns from South Carolina, Florida, and Louisiana. In hindsight it seems clear that his opponent, Democrat Samuel Tilden, was entitled at least to the Florida vote, and this by itself would have been enough to ensure Tilden's victory. Disputed results, a disputed electoral commission, and a filibuster followed in Congress, delaying the vote count. The filibuster was finally broken by a seamy bargain according to which enough Southern Democrats abandoned the filibuster to allow Hayes to be elected president—provided federal troops were removed from the Southern states, where they had remained to guarantee the political and civil rights of the freed blacks. The compromise was brokered through intermediaries, and the extent of an explicit bargain has been disputed. "But no one disputes that . . . the effect was to nullify the rights won by black Americans through the Fourteenth and Fifteenth Amendments."[26]

Under these dispiriting circumstances, Booker T. Washington emerged as an advocate of "industrial education" for blacks. Founder of the Tuskegee Institute, he came forward as a leader under the banner of what came to be known as the "Atlanta compromise": "In all things purely social we can be as separate as the five fingers and yet one as the hand in all things essential to mutual progress."[27] As his critic W. E. B. Du Bois noted in his path-breaking book, *The Souls of Black Folk,* published in 1903, "To-day he stands as the one recognized spokesman of his ten million fellows, and one of the most notable figures in a nation of seventy millions."[28]

Du Bois had no quarrel with the virtues Washington was promulgating. "So far as Mr. Washington preaches Thrift, Prudence, and Industrial Training for the masses, we must hold up his hands and strive with him." However, "so far as Mr. Washington apologizes for injustice, North or South, does not rightly value the privilege and duty of voting, belittles the emasculating effects of caste distinctions and opposes the higher training and ambition of our brighter minds . . . we must unceasingly and firmly oppose them." Du Bois objected to Washington's program because it "asks that people give up" political power, "insistence on civil rights," and higher education. Instead, Washington asked blacks to focus on "industrial education, the accumulation of wealth and the conciliation with the South." The result had been, in the period since 1877, a steady disfranchisement, "the legal creation of a distinct status of civil inferiority," and even a lessening of support for higher education for blacks.[29]

Du Bois's argument for higher educational aspirations for blacks was a strategy for overcoming what he called the "veil," the social limitations on self-understanding that had created the Negro of the old South—"a clownish, simple creature, at times even lovable within its limitations, but strictly foreordained to walk within the Veil." Perhaps in self-defense, the old South had wrapped around blacks "a veil so thick that they *shall not even think* of breaking through" (emphasis added). Du Bois writes both within and outside this veil: "I who speak here am bone of the bone and flesh of the flesh of them that live within the Veil." Du Bois grapples with a double consciousness, a double identity. "The Negro is a sort of seventh son, born with a veil, and gifted with a second-sight in this American world." He experiences "a peculiar sensation, this double-consciousness, this sense of always looking at one's self through the eyes of others, of measuring one's soul by the tape of a world that looks on in amused contempt and pity. One ever feels his two-ness—an American, a Negro; two souls; two thoughts, two unreconciled strivings, two warring ideals in one dark body, whose dogged strength alone keeps it from being torn asunder."[30]

Through learning, there may be the possibility of transcending the veil and the double consciousness it creates. Du Bois closes his essay on "The Training of Black Men" with the moving image of his sitting with Shakespeare without experiencing any condescension, of his transcending the color line, "wed with truth": "I sit with Shakespeare and he winces not. Across the color line I move arm in arm with Balzac and Dumas, where smiling men and welcoming women glide in gilded halls. . . . I summon Aristotle and Aurelius and what soul I will and they come all graciously with no scorn nor condescension. So, wed with Truth, I dwell above the Veil. Is this the life you grudge us, O knightly America?"[31]

Du Bois also felt he could appeal directly to the declared principles of this knightly America. Like Frederick Douglass before him, he could best clinch the argument for full civil and political equality by invoking the Declaration of Independence. He closes his long critique of the policies of Booker T. Washington, policies that were dominant at the time, by declaring:

By every civilized and peaceful method we must strive for the rights which the world accords to men, clinging unwaveringly to those great words which the sons of the Fathers would fain forget: "We hold these truths to be self-evident: that all men are created equal; that they are endowed by their Creator with certain inalienable rights; that among these are life, liberty and the pursuit of happiness."[32]

THE QUEST FOR VOTING EQUALITY

The complexity of the impediments to black voting equality were noted by the most distinguished foreign observer ever to visit America, Alexis de Tocqueville. In a footnote in his celebrated *Democracy in America,* he recalled this exchange with "a Pennsylvanian" during his travels around America in 1831–1832. "Please explain to me why in a state founded by Quakers and renowned for its tolerance, freed negroes are not allowed to use their rights as citizens? They pay taxes; is it not right that they should vote?"

The Pennsylvanian replied that it was an "insult" to think that the legislators in a state like Pennsylvania would have deprived blacks of the vote. Tocqueville expressed puzzlement: if blacks had the right, why had he seen none of them voting? The response was: "That is not the fault of the law. It is true that Negroes have the right to be present at elections, but they voluntarily abstain from appearing." Tocqueville thought this "extraordinarily modest of them" but was corrected. "Oh! it is not that they are reluctant to go there, but they are afraid they may be maltreated." For "the majority is filled with the strongest prejudices against Negroes, and the magistrates do not feel strong enough to guarantee the rights granted to them by the lawmakers."[33]

Blacks had been given the right on paper, but the informal social impediments to voting and political power could be overwhelming, even in the relatively tolerant North. Hearts had to be changed for rights to be effective. In the South, even the rights blacks acquired on paper were rolled back. The brief flowering of black political enfranchisement after the Civil War was quickly followed by the reimposition of legal barriers after the end of Reconstruction. By the time Du Bois was writing, a host of new legal as well as social impediments had been introduced.

Writing at the turn of the century, around the same time as Du Bois, Charles W. Chesnutt, a noted black novelist, offered a systematic account of the new impediments constructed to prevent blacks from exercising their right to vote, a right by then enshrined in the Constitution. The new barriers, which had developed in various Southern states, mostly in the period since 1876, were of three main types. First, there were seemingly objective limitations that, if they were applied to all citizens equally, might lead, Chesnutt observed, to a defensible version of a restricted franchise. These limitations were a property qualification, the required payment of a poll tax, and an educational qualification: voters must be able to read and write. Chesnutt noted that these qualifications, although they might apply disproportionately to blacks, would not by themselves deprive blacks of effective representation.

There was a second group of limitations, however, that contained an "understanding" clause typified by the one in a Mississippi statute that required a voter to be able "to read, or understand when read to him, any clause in the Constitution." As Chesnutt notes, these qualifications "are left to the discretion and judgment of the registering officer."[34]

When this discretionary requirement was combined with inherited qualifications, the effect was the disfranchisement of black citizens and enfranchisement of whites. Various prescriptive qualifications appeared in voting laws, such as the one in North Carolina that "the descendant of any person who had the right to vote on January 1, 1867, inherits that right" or the one in Alabama that any descendant of a soldier would have the right to vote. These qualifications helped define "a privileged class of permanently enrolled voters not subject to any of the other restrictions," concludes Chesnutt (85).

These restrictions had the powerful result of effectively disfranchising black voters. "The colored people are left . . . absolutely without representation, direct or indirect, in any law-making body, in any court of justice, in any branch of government" (88). Even though they constitute a majority in several Southern states and make up one-eighth of the population of the country as a whole, Chesnutt argues, blacks are not able "to send one representative to the Congress." They "have not direct representation in any Southern legislature, and no voice in determining the choice of white men who might be friendly to their rights. Nor are they able to influence the election of judges or other public officials, to whom are entrusted the protection of their lives, their liberties and their property." Left without any political power, they are victimized by a host of illegal acts of violent intimidation. "Day after day the catalogue of lynchings and anti-Negro riots upon every imaginable pretext grows longer and more appalling." Given this picture of the plight of the disfranchised black, Chesnutt can only conclude that the "country stands face to face with the revival of slavery" (89).

The "negro is subjected to taxation without representation"—a violation of rights that "the forefathers of this Republic made the basis of a bloody revolution" (90). Worse, "the white South sends to Congress, on a basis including the Negro population, a delegation nearly twice as large as it is justly entitled to, and one which may always safely be relied upon to oppose in Congress every measure which seeks to protect the equality, or to enlarge the rights of colored citizens" (93).

There is only one compensation remaining, "the sole remnant" of what blacks "acquired through the civil war, a very inadequate public school education." But considering the kind of education the black man was offered, and the opportunities available later, it is as if the white South had said to him, "Behold how good a friend I am of yours! Have I not left you a stomach and a pair of arms, and will I not generously permit you to work for me with the one, that you may thereby

115

gain enough to fill the other? A brain you do not need. We will relieve you of any responsibility that might seem to demand such an organ" (95–96).

Chesnutt held out eventual hope from three tribunals: the courts, Congress, and public opinion. The key, he speculated, would be public opinion over the long term, for the moral case was on the side of justice for blacks. "There is, somewhere in the Universe a 'Power that works for righteousness' and that leads men to do justice to one another. To this power, working on the hearts and consciences of men, the Negro can always appeal" (124).

Public opinion took a long time to bring about an effective realization of voting rights. In the 1940s, when political scientist V. O. Key wrote his classic analysis of Southern politics, the situation was largely unchanged. Even by the early 1960s, on the eve of what became the landmark Voting Rights Act proposed by Lyndon Johnson, the access of blacks to the ballot was extremely limited in many Southern states. The public policy specialist Abigail Thernstrom notes that while only 3 percent of Georgia blacks were registered to vote in 1940, by 1964 the level had still reached only 27.4 percent. In South Carolina, it had reached only 37.3 percent. There were only two Southern states in which as many as half of the blacks were registered.[35] There were still serious legal and social impediments to the exercise of the rights that had, almost a century before, been guaranteed on paper by the Fifteenth Amendment.

Chesnutt had predicted in 1903 that the intransigence of Southern whites would provoke a change from the rest of the country, just as it had earlier provoked the Civil War.[36] It took more than sixty years, but Chesnutt's speculation came true. As Thernstrom summarizes the breakthrough on voting rights, "Overt resistance . . . was the white South's fatal error. In March 1965, an outraged nation watched Selma police assault blacks and whites marching to secure the right of citizens to vote. Eight days later President Johnson went on national television to urge new legislation and on August 6 he signed the Voting

Rights Act into law."[37] National television coverage helped crystallize public opinion, and the moral appeal to that opinion provided a new basis for inclusion and political participation.

The Voting Rights Act brought about a dramatic change in registration. Within two years the percentage of blacks who were registered to vote jumped from less than 7 percent to 60 percent in Mississippi. From 1964 to 1967 the number of blacks registered to vote in the eleven Southern states jumped by 45 percent, from 2 million to 2.9 million. From 1964 to 1970 the percentage of voting-age blacks who were registered in those states increased from 40 percent to 70 percent.[38]

Yet voting, by itself, does not necessarily bring political representation. A variety of racial gerrymandering techniques served, for a time, to dilute or deny voting power to blacks. The term *gerrymander* comes from the action of the majority party in Massachusetts in 1812, which drew boundaries to split up Essex County and thus dilute the power of the Federalists. The early American portrait painter Gilbert Stuart coined the term, which derived from Governor Eldridge Gerry, who approved the Massachusetts plan. It alluded to the fact that the district, with its strange new boundaries, looked like a salamander.[39] It resembled one even more closely after Stuart embellished a map of the district with a head and claws.[40]

Four techniques of racial gerrymandering blunted the initial force of black registration. These four techniques were the creation of "at-large" districts, "cracking," "stacking," and "packing."

At-large voting means that a number of legislators are elected from a particular district; the minority can thus be outvoted in each race and receive no representation at all. In Hinds County, Mississippi, for example, the most populous county in the state, a series of state legislative reapportionment plans required that all twelve representatives and all five state senators be chosen at large. Even though blacks constituted 40 percent of the population countywide they were effectively shut out of the process, despite high voter registration. They did not achieve representation until 1975, when the at-large system was abandoned and single-member districts were required in a court-ordered plan.[41]

But single-member districting is not, by itself, enough to guarantee any representation. That depends on how the districts are drawn. "Cracking" occurs when a minority concentration is divided up and shared by several adjacent districts. Frank Parker describes how the Mississippi legislature reacted to the registration of blacks after the Voting Rights Act. "Just as blacks were beginning to register and vote, the Mississippi legislature in 1966 redrew the congressional district lines horizontally, along an east-west configuration, dismembering the heavy black population concentration in the Delta, and split it up among four of the five congressional districts. All five districts were majority white in voting age population."[42]

"Stacking" occurs when a large minority population is combined with an even larger adjacent population so that the minority votes become diluted. This happened in Macon County, Alabama. Macon, with a sizable nonwhite population, was combined with two largely white counties in a redistricting plan that was passed in Alabama just six weeks after the Voting Rights Act. Booker T. Washington, the founding father of the Tuskegee Institute—located in Macon County—had urged blacks to be patient in their quest for the vote. He predicted in *Up from Slavery,* in 1901, that it would come in time. Sixty-four years later, the stacking of his district was litigated by the courts in *Sims v. Badget.*[43] Even with the vote achieved, gerrymandering could rob voters in his home district of any meaningful influence.

"Packing" occurs when minorities are overconcentrated in a single district to limit the number of representatives they can elect. Parker found the pattern occurring in several states, beginning with the New York congressional redistricting plan that was challenged in 1961 in *Wright v. Rockefeller:* "The New York legislators packed black and Puerto Rican voters into one of four Manhattan congressional districts, where, combined, they comprised 86 percent of the population, leaving minority voters only 29 percent, 28 percent and 5 percent of the population in the adjoining districts."[44] If minorities are overconcentrated, or packed, into districts to a much higher degree than they need to elect a representative (say, at the 80 percent level), then they have less influence on the adjacent districts.

The federal government had a basis for monitoring these efforts to rob registered blacks of representation. Districts that were covered under the Voting Rights Act fell under a provision of "preclearance"— they needed to check with federal authorities before they altered any of their voting procedures. The Voting Rights Act was also explicitly amended in 1982 to deal with questions of vote dilution.[45] Over time, these provisions gave federal officials enough power to bring about significant minority representation.

Abigail Thernstrom illustrates the progress blacks have made by quoting this Alabama political advertisement from 1981: "Before we had the right to vote, politicians publicly called us niggers. After we received the right to vote, but our numbers were few, they called us Nigras. When we reached 5,000, they called us colored. 10,000, they called us black people. Now that we have reached 50,000, they call us Commissioner Wicks, Judge Cain Kennedy, Representative Yvonne Kennedy and Senator Figures."[46] At this writing, there are now more than 8,000 black elected officials nationwide.

But progress in electing minorities to the U.S. Congress came slowly. As late as 1981–1982, fifteen years after the passage of the original Voting Rights Act, "the southern congressional delegation, consisting of 108 representatives, contained only two blacks, although 20 percent of the region's population was black. Mississippi, Alabama and Georgia, with black populations of 35 percent, 26 percent and 27 percent, respectively, had no black congresspersons among their twenty-two representatives."[47] Yet within another decade, by the 1990s, the Congressional Black Caucus contained forty members and had become a significant force on Capitol Hill.

But the Voting Rights Act had significant partisan political consequences. Take Georgia. In the early 1980s ten of the eleven congress-men were Democrats and there was one Republican, Newt Gingrich. After the 1994 election, there were seven Republicans and only four Democrats, but three of the four Democrats were in minority districts created under the Voting Rights Act. The Voting Rights Act may have had the twofold effect of further identifying minority interests with the Democratic Party, especially in the South, and of concentrating mi-nority votes in "safe" districts, leaving the Republicans to benefit dis-proportionately from the remaining white districts, which were often in suburban areas.

A further problem is that in many minority districts, the Democratic primary becomes the only election that counts because the general election will not be competitively contested by Republicans. As a re-sult, minority turnout in general elections is lowered in these districts, since there are no significant contests for the representatives minorities care most about.

There is no easy solution to these problems. As long as there is a pattern of racial block voting, and as long as we maintain an electoral system of geographically based districts, the issue of how those dis-tricts are drawn must be confronted. This issue has become particu-larly thorny in recent court cases. In *Shaw v. Reno* the Supreme Court set aside a district that snaked around the state of North Carolina along a major highway on the grounds that it was so bizarre that it could only have been drawn on racial grounds. The majority wrote: "In some exceptional cases, a reapportionment plan may be so highly ir-regular that, on its face, it rationally cannot be understood as anything other than an effort to 'segregate . . . voters.' "[48] When the boundaries lack "traditional districting principles such as compactness, contiguity and respect for political subdivisions" then, even though these criteria are not Constitutionally required, the question arises whether "a dis-trict has been gerrymandered on racial lines." A sufficiently "ugly" dis-trict becomes suspect, although "ugly" has never been well defined.[49]

But the Voting Rights Act requires the creation of districts where blacks can be confident of winning, even though a districting plan that is obviously engineered along racial lines can be thrown out as a racial gerrymander. The Court is wrestling with incompatible requirements and unclear precedents. Some of the problems were highlighted by the earlier case of *United Jewish Organization of Williamsburgh v. Carey* (1977). The Williamsburgh section of Brooklyn had always had its own representation in the state legislature, representation that served a constituency of Hasidic Jews. In 1974 the New York legislature divided this area up because the state's redistricting plan had an insufficient number of safe minority (nonwhite) districts. The Hasidic Jews experienced the cracking of their district. The Court, however, treated the Jews just as one more nonminority group with no special claim to being represented. Harking back to notions of "virtual representation" that would have enraged the Founding Fathers, the Court speculated that the Jews would be represented by white legislators elected from other districts. As Justice White said, speaking for the Court, the plan "left white majorities in approximately 70 percent of the assembly and senate districts in Kings County which had a countywide population that was 65 percent white. . . . Whites would not be underrepresented relative to their share of the population." Presumably, the Irish and Italian legislators elected elsewhere in Brooklyn would represent the Hasidic Jews of Williamsburgh.[50]

So long as there are geographical districts and racial or ethnic block voting, the districting process will create predictable winners and losers. If districts are created to ensure minority winners, then there will be nonminority losers. If districts are created to ensure white winners, then there will be nonwhite losers. Some day we may aspire to a system where whites are willing to vote for blacks and vice versa. We see signs of this in white support which permitted the election of candidates such as Governor Douglas Wilder of Virginia and Mayor David Dinkins of New York. If blacks also become less predictable in their voting patterns, supporting occasional Republicans as well as Democrats, then the dilemmas of racial districting will disappear.

Until then, the effort to produce minority representation as well as minority votes means that there will be predictable losers as well as predictable winners.

An alternative would be to develop a different voting system. Proportional representation would remove the problem of drawing geographical boundaries and better translate votes into seats for any particular group. But proportional representation would break the tie between a candidate and her district. Arguably, there is a specific kind of accountability produced when we know that our congressional and our state legislators are responsible for helping the people in our district. Given the way that the American system has developed, any such drastic change in our voting system seems an unlikely reform. In the meantime, the geographical contortions of the gerrymander will probably continue to affect whose votes actually produce seats in our legislative bodies.

THE DECLARATION OF SENTIMENTS

In April 1776, while Congress was debating the Declaration of Independence, Abigail Adams wrote to her husband, John, a member of the drafting committee of the Declaration: "Remember, all men would be tyrants if they could. If particular care and attention is not paid to the ladies we are determined to foment a rebellion and will not hold ourselves bound by any laws in which we have no voice or representation."[51] Just as the signers of the Declaration had held that they were subject to tyrannous laws in which they had no real voice, Abigail Adams held that women were subject to tyranny without proper representation. In this she was identifying a need to be included in the rights of the Declaration.

Her letter was answered with gallantry but no concessions by her husband (a future president of the United States). A far more obscure convention some seventy years later, however, laid the groundwork for the eventual realization of Abigail Adams's demand.

In 1840 the newly married Elizabeth Cady Stanton of New York accompanied her husband on a trip to London to attend the World Anti-Slavery Conference. Women had long been active in the anti-slavery movement, a movement that was more socially acceptable than the nascent women's movement. In this case, as in others, the catalyst for raising the issue of inclusion was a convention in which some voices could not be heard and that some people could not enter.

Just as women and blacks were certainly left out of the deliberations of Congress and of the Constitutional Convention, the young Elizabeth Cady Stanton found, on arrival at the Freemason's Hall in London, that female delegates were not permitted to take part in the debate. She later wrote in her autobiography that this was the beginning of her commitment to women's rights. Like the slaves she wished to free, women were treated as another class of beings, one that was not permitted to speak for itself. At the convention, they were relegated to a position behind a screen from which they were permitted to listen to the debates, where they were joined by the abolitionist William Lloyd Garrison, who shared their indignation at their exclusion.[52]

Years later, in a speech to another Anti-Slavery Convention, Stanton would remember how "nobly Garrison would not speak, because woman was there denied her rights. Think of a World's Convention and one half of the world left out!" Of the anti-slavery activists who also spoke for women's rights she says: "All time would not be long enough to pay the debt of gratitude we owe these noble men, who spoke for us when we were dumb, who roused us to a sense of our own rights, to the dignity of our high calling." Once aroused, she saw her mission, and that of the Anti-Slavery Society, as devotion "not to the African slave alone, but to the slaves of custom, creed and sex, as well."[53]

Segregated from the men at the convention, Stanton met Lucretia Mott, another American delegate, who impressed her as the first woman in her experience "who had sufficient confidence in herself to frame and hold an opinion in the face of opposition."[54] They talked about the proceedings of the convention and also about the rights of women. There, they laid the basis for a friendship that would energize the American women's movement. Stanton had long been interested in women's rights, but she had lacked an opportunity to pursue her convictions. As a seven-year-old, she had attempted with scissors to cut laws discriminating against women out of her father's law books.[55] But her consciousness was not fully awakened until she was excluded from the London convention and made the acquaintance of Mott.

Eight years later, after having given birth to three children, Stanton received a visit from Mott at her home in Seneca Falls, New York. The visit sparked an excited series of conversations and led to their decision to call a convention of their own to discuss women's rights. They wrote an advertisement for the local paper, the *Seneca Court Courier,* announcing "A convention to discuss the social, civil and religious condition and rights of woman."

Stanton proposed that the convention draw up a declaration modeled on the Declaration of Independence. Abigail Adams's request that women be included in the inalienable rights of the first declaration found eventual fulfillment in a document drafted in an obscure gathering in a small New York town some seventy years later. But the moral force of the idea had a simple and compelling logic. It also gave focus and visibility to the convention and helped to justify the convention's most controversial proposal—woman's suffrage: "It is the duty of the women of this country to secure to themselves their sacred right to the elective franchise."[56]

In making her case for adopting the Declaration of Sentiments, Stanton rejected claims that women were already represented. The same doctrine of virtual representation—the notion that those who were elected would consider the interests of all the people, even of those who could not vote—that the American Founders had to confront in arguing that they were not properly represented in the British Parliament had to be confronted by women. " 'But you are already represented by your fathers, husbands, brothers and sons?' Let your statute books answer the question. We have had enough of such representation."[57]

Stanton's declaration had the same structure as the original. "We hold these truths to be self-evident: that all men and women are created equal; that they are endowed by their Creator with certain inalienable rights; that among these are life, liberty and the pursuit of happiness." Abuse of these God-given rights is catalogued, and remedies are proposed. "The history of mankind is a history of repeated injuries and usurpations on the part of man toward woman, having in direct object the establishment of an absolute tyranny over her." First among the abuses is denial of the "inalienable right to the elective franchise." As a result, each woman is denied a voice in the laws to which she must submit; she is denied "representation in the halls of legislation"; and she is denied various other rights, most notably rights to property, employment, and education. And man has even "endeavoured, in every way that he could, to destroy her confidence in her own powers, to lessen her self-respect, and to make her willing to lead a dependent and abject life."[58]

As a remedy, the declaration demands that women be admitted "to all the rights and privileges that belong to them as citizens of the United States." A list of particular resolutions follows, including, most notably, the right to vote. But the authors state that the relegation of woman to a special sphere has been such that they feel it necessary to ask that women be permitted to address public gatherings without "the objection of indelicacy and impropriety" and that recognition be granted that "woman is man's equal—was intended to be so by the Creator."[59]

The convention attracted wide attention and ridicule, but it articulated the moral foundations of the women's movement and helped lay the groundwork for the eventual realization of the vote for women. Stanton, who formed a working partnership with suffragist Susan B. Anthony, devoted her life to the cause, but failed to live to see its full realization. As a writer and speaker, however, she ably articulated the case for the inclusion of women to the same fundamental rights as men. As she argued some forty years after the Declaration of Sentiments, "Surely the mothers who rocked the cradle for this Republic may be safely trusted to sustain their sires and sons in all their best efforts to establish in the New World a government to which the sound principles of our Constitution and Declaration of Independence may be fully realized, in which there shall be no privileged classes, but equal rights for all."[60]

Anthony made similar speeches. In words reminiscent of the case Frederick Douglass made for blacks, she would quote the Constitution as well as the Declaration of Independence and comment: "It was we, the people, not we, the white male citizens, not we the male citizens, but we, the whole people, who formed this Union." The idea was to secure the liberties, "not to the half of ourselves and the half of our posterity, but to the whole people, women as well as men."[61]

The vision did not achieve full realization of voting rights until passage of the Nineteenth Amendment in 1920. Neither Elizabeth Cady Stanton nor Susan B. Anthony lived to see it, but they had started the National Women's Suffrage Association, a forerunner of the organization that finally helped realize those voting rights (the National American Woman Suffrage Association [NAWSA]). More important, they articulated the moral argument for inclusion, on the basis of fundamental American ideals, in a manner that served to expand the application of democratic rights to half the population.

WHOSE AMERICA?
HOW DO WE COME TO SUPPORT IT?

The city of San Jose, California, the nation's twelfth largest city, commissioned a statue of Capt. Thomas Fallon, the nineteenth-century soldier who first raised the U.S. flag over San Jose in 1846. In 1990, protests by Hispanic citizens' groups led to the statue's being mothballed until it could be paired with "four additional statues each depicting the history of a different segment of this diverse area," according to one press report.[62] But one of the additional statues, a Plumed Serpent representing the Aztec god Quetzalcoatl, has been vigorously protested by some devout Christian Latino groups because it is a pagan image connected with human sacrifice. "Even though it's part of the culture, it is still demonic. We wish not to be represented this way," says Manuel Salazar, a local Latino artist involved in one of the protests.[63] The proposal for the four additional statues is enmeshed in the debate: "Indian sculpture for the north gateway to commemorate the first settlers. Pioneer art for the east because that's where the covered wagons came from. Asian art for the west, to recognize the newest immigrant's route. And Mexican art for the south."[64]

In the midst of this debate, what happened to Capt. Fallon? Journalists have had a field day with the fact that no one can locate the controversial statue. "I think he's in the witness relocation program," commented former Mayor Tom McEnery, once one of the statue's key defenders.

The San Jose statues symbolize an important problem: To whose heritage and whose America do we commit ourselves? The same forces that have enlarged our democracy and widened our elective franchise have also made our conception of ourselves and our history more inclusive. As we reconceptualize our collective identity, the earlier forces of exclusion lose their power. But in this diversity we also have increasing difficulty in finding the cultural symbols that can unite us. As the symbols change, how we commit ourselves to the Republic changes as well. The sources of loyalty and of moral authority are inextricably connected to symbols of the heritage that binds us together.

Anna Julia Cooper, an educator and writer in the 1890s, ruminated on these questions in her classic *A Voice from the South.* "America for Americans!" her essay cried out satirically. "This is the white man's country! The Chinese must go, shrieks the exclusionist. Exclude the Italians! Colonize the blacks in Mexico or deport them to Africa."[65]

But the question " 'Who are Americans?' comes rolling back from ten million throats." How is such a question to be answered? "Who are the homefolks and who are the strangers? Who are the absolute and original tenants in fee-simple?" Cooper notes that the Indians "are at least the oldest inhabitants of whom we can at present identify any traces" and that when the *Mayflower* landed, there had already been the "first delegation from Africa just one year ahead ... in 1619." (She is here referring to the first slave ship to arrive at Jamestown). If we are to keep "America for Americans" then "at least the cleavage cannot be made by hues and noses."[66]

Given this diversity, "there never was a time since America became a nation when there were not more than one race, more than one party, more than one belief contending for supremacy." What holds us together, from the Declaration of Independence on, is "a general amnesty and universal reciprocity" and a capacity for "compromise and concession, liberality and toleration." These allow "the only *modus vivendi* in a nation whose every citizen is his own king, his own priest and his own pope."[67]

But toleration and compromise do not inspire veneration. A working arrangement, a modus vivendi, where people go about their own business inspires limited loyalty. Perhaps the values of the Constitution and the Declaration of Independence have served, in some periods, to provide more unity and collective identity. But studies show that most citizens know little and do not support, when asked, many of the key principles in the Constitution.[68] They support the symbol without knowing much about its contents.[69]

The Founders held that government required a certain "veneration" to maintain itself. This veneration would come partly from time and partly from shared opinion. Madison, in *Federalist* no. 49, worried that without veneration, "the wisest and freest governments would not possess the requisite stability." He held that "all governments rest on opinion." And "when the examples that fortify opinion are ancient as well as numerous, they are known to have a double effect." Ancient examples are important because of "that veneration which time bestows on everything." Numerous examples matter because "the reason of man . . . is timid and cautious when left alone, and acquires firmness and confidence in proportion to the number with which it is associated."

Hence, history is the battleground for veneration and loyalty in support of the political system. In *Federalist* no. 49 Madison mentions one exception. "In a nation of philosophers, this consideration ought to be disregarded. A reverence for the laws would be sufficiently inculcated by the voice of an enlightened reason." But this theoretical solution is unrealistic. "A nation of philosophers is as little to be expected as the philosophical race of kings wished for by Plato."

Early in this century, the British monarchy, the official descendant of the institution from which we declared our independence, faced fundamentally the same problem: how to maintain the support of a greatly enlarged—and increasingly diverse—mass of subjects once the voting franchise was enlarged, once literacy had spread, and once the British public began to act as citizens as well as subjects. The British solution was the *invention* of tradition, combined with its promulgation by the new technologies that were just becoming available. As historian David Cannadine notes: "Between the late 1870s and 1914 . . . there was a fundamental change in the public image of the British monarch, as its ritual, hitherto inept, private and of limited appeal, became splendid, public and popular." With new communications and transportation and the social changes they brought—"a widening franchise, the railway, the steamship, the telegraph, electricity, the tram"—the monarchy had to reach out in new ways to support the " 'preservation of anachronism,' the deliberate, ceremonial presentation of an impotent but venerated monarch as a unifying symbol of permanence and national community." The growth of the mass press, the development of photography, and, most important, the development of radio and television were all crucial. Coronations, weddings, funerals all took on a grandeur unknown before the age of the mass media. New occasions and new ceremonials were invented. The deliberately archaic presentation of events created the impression of ancient and continuous traditions where, in fact, none had existed. At the coronation of George VI, for example, all but three of the peers arrived in automobiles, but by the coronation of Queen Elizabeth II, in 1953, so many horse-drawn coaches had to be found for the televised proceedings that many had to be borrowed from a film company.[70]

Radio and later television brought an audience of millions to what had once been occasions for a privileged few:

> From the time of the Duke of York's wedding in 1923, "audible pageants" became a permanent feature of the B.B.C.'s programmes, as each great state occasion was broadcast live on the radio, with special microphones positioned so that the listener could hear the sound of bells, horses, carriages and cheering. In a very real sense, it was this technical development which made possible the successful presentation of state pageants as national, family events, in which everyone could take part. . . . Record audiences were a constant feature of the outside broadcasts of great royal occasions.[71]

The invention of tradition was not unique to Britain. Bastille Day, the commemoration of the French Revolution of 1789, was not invented until 1880. But the British adapted the new technologies of press, radio, and photography to create a veneration that, for a time, seemed to embody national identity. More recently, the same forces of tabloidization and sensationalism that we found infecting American politics have, perhaps, led the Royal family to regret its openness to the media. A functioning royalty, even in a limited constitutional monarchy, is not the same as celebrity, and many private revelations may well undermine moral legitimacy.

American heads of state can have the same problems with a tabloid press, as President Clinton well knows, but American presidents do not embody the nation in the same way as the British monarch, who presumes to be above all partisan divisions. Although we have had our "imperial presidencies," we need to look elsewhere for any continuing sense of national identity.[72] What symbols or methods do we have to inculcate the unity and support that could legitimate the system and give it a firm basis in the continuing consent of the public?

This question is closely connected to another: What kinds of citizens do we want? Madison concludes his meditation on this problem by noting (in *Federalist* no. 49) that without a nation of philosophers, "the most rational government will not find it a superfluous advantage to have the prejudices of the community on its side." A nation of philosophers is certainly unrealistic, but should a government, born in liberty, teach its people to revere those same liberties?

We have no monarch; we may disagree on statues; but in our diverse society, there are, nevertheless, a few common symbols of sufficient emotional power to attract the loyalty or veneration that Madison had in mind—the Declaration of Independence, the Constitution, the flag. We can focus the problem by looking at the classic debate over the role of the state in inculcating loyalty to itself by insisting that children salute the flag.

Between 1940 and 1943 there were two dramatic Supreme Court cases on the issue, and they posed the question of the limits of the state's authority to inculcate support for itself. Both cases involved children who, on religious grounds, did not wish to salute the flag. But neither case was treated as one centrally concerned with freedom of religion. The question was whether the state can compel a profession of belief in order to instill veneration or a habit of support. Justice Felix Frankfurter, writing for the Court in the first case, *Minersville v. Gobitis,* held that it could. Justice Robert H. Jackson, writing three years later in the second case, *Board of Education v. Barnette,* held that it could not.

Frankfurter's premise was that "the ultimate foundation of a free society is the binding tie of cohesive sentiment. Such a sentiment is fostered by all those agencies of the mind and spirit which may serve to gather up the traditions of a people, transmit them from generation to generation, and thereby create that continuity of a treasured common life which constitutes a civilization." Frankfurter argued that "personal freedom is best maintained" when "it is ingrained in a people's habits." A state "may in self-protection utilize the educational process for inculcating those almost unconscious feelings which bind men together in a comprehending loyalty."[73]

Following Frankfurter's decision, the state of West Virginia passed legislation that required the "teaching, fostering and perpetuating [of] the ideals, principles and spirit of Americanism." In addition to curricular changes, the Board of Education responded to the new legislation by requiring that students pledge allegiance to the flag. Failure to conform was deemed insubordination and dealt with by expulsion. A suit was brought on behalf of Jehovah's Witness children, who regarded saluting the flag as deference to a graven image and hence prohibited by their religion.

Once again, the issue was not religious freedom, in particular, but the more general freedoms of speech and conscience. Justice Jackson, writing for the Court, argued that "we are dealing with the compulsion of a student to declare a belief." He contrasted two means of instilling loyalty. One was making students informed and aware, the other was enforcing a routine. The students "are not merely made acquainted with the flag salute so that they may be informed as to what it is or even what it means. The issue is whether this slow and easily neglected route to aroused loyalties constitutionally may be short-cut by substituting a compulsory salute and slogan."[74] Jackson did not quarrel with Frankfurter's end of national unity. He only questioned "whether under our Constitution compulsion as here employed is a permissible means for its achievement." In the throes of World War II, when the country faced the threat of totalitarianism, he noted the failure of attempts to coerce uniformity of opinion, from the Roman efforts to stamp out Christianity to "the Siberian exiles as a means to Russian unity."

Rather than use the shortcut of compulsory indoctrination, Jackson held out the hope that "consent of the governed" could be maintained amid diversity of opinion. Government can rest on the "appeal of our institutions to free minds" rather than on "compulsory routine." In inspiring words, he defended the freedom not to be instructed in what to believe: "If there is any fixed star in our constitutional constellation, it is that no official, high or petty, can prescribe what shall be orthodox in politics, nationalism, religion or other matters of opinion or force citizens to confess by word or act of faith therein."[75]

The Court overturned its earlier decision and affirmed the right of students not to pledge allegiance to the flag. In so doing, the Court eschewed the shortcut to loyalty that would come from repetitive and compulsory affirmations of allegiance. The irony is that few students in public schools avail themselves of the opportunity to opt out. Most simply comply with the ceremony and pledge their allegiance. Since this classic debate unfolded in the two Supreme Court decisions, many tens of millions of students have continued to be subjected to the daily routine of saluting the flag and pledging allegiance. We thus affirm in principle the right of people to opt out of the process, but we get the benefit of the compulsory routine because only a minuscule portion ever think to exercise this Constitutionally protected right. Should we seek, as Frankfurter argued, the "binding tie of cohesive sentiment" through inculcation—through what Madison called "veneration"—or should we consider such practices a shortcut compared to the "slow and easily neglected route" by which informed citizens come to support their government—the very government that protects their liberty of thought? The second route suggests the utopian aspiration Madison identified as the achievement of a nation of "philosophers." Governments would not have to rest on "prejudice" if all citizens were philosophers. Or, lacking a citizenry of philosophers, is it possible to do more than we have to create a public of engaged and thoughtful citizens? Is there a better way to achieve a public that thinks for itself just enough to live up to Justice Jackson's aspiration—"Authority here is to be controlled by public opinion, not public opinion by authority."[76]

5

GIVING THE PEOPLE VOICE

When do the people speak authoritatively about their form of government? At a Constitutional convention, is the official and distinctively American answer. Elected delegates from the entire polity gather together in a single place and, like the American Founders, they deliberate on a structure of government. They engage in face-to-face debate, they air competing arguments, and they vote on specific provisions, which are then taken in some way to the rest of the people. But Constitutional conventions are rare events. And the ideal of face-to-face democracy has found other methods of realization, some as influential as official conventions.

In 1894 the state of New York held its own constitutional convention, but the event was instructive in showing how those who are left out can eventually acquire a voice. In both England and America there was a long tradition of "virtual representation"—the notion according to which those who could not vote or participate were nevertheless represented because members of Parliament, or members of legislatures, would consider the interests of everyone. But Americans during the Revolution would have none of virtual representation. It was not good enough for our Founders. And there were later groups, blacks and women, who came to reject such arguments as well.

One such group of women had just failed to convince the New

York state constitutional convention in 1894. They petitioned from outside, but they did not believe that the men inside would consider their interests and grant them the vote. After a long campaign, they gathered together in New York City on a snowy morning and decided to change tactics. Instead of circulating further petitions for the vote, they formed an organization devoted to education and discussion. It was called the League for Political Education. Later it changed its name to Town Hall, and it sponsored one of the first constructive efforts to use the mass media for serious public deliberation.

The six women who had failed to convince the New York constitutional convention that women should have the vote attempted to achieve power through discussion. Their idea was to create a public space where women as well as men could be included in the discussion of public affairs. Given the "separate sphere" in which women were expected to live, this was a considerable innovation. And it helped give birth to another. The beginning of serious talk radio, the show "America's Town Meeting of the Air" sponsored by their organization, had its roots in the group's recognition of the power of face-to-face discussion and the importance of including everyone in the debate. Women could not vote, so they attempted to adapt the New England town meeting to the giant city of New York—to create new "town meetings" and other public events where women could be included on an equal basis. Power through discussion would lay the groundwork for achieving the vote, but it would also provide the educational preparation that would permit that vote to make a difference.

In the mid-1930s a young innovator, George V. Denny, became the associate director of the League for Political Education and decided that what it had attempted in New York City could be enlarged further, via the new medium of radio, to the entire nation. In an analysis that anticipated the deficiencies of mass democracy, Denny grappled with the problem of how the mass media, the newspapers and radio of the period, had failed to further citizen deliberation. He observed that citizens commonly listened to, and read, views with which they agreed.

They seemed to form their opinions without attention to the arguments offered by opposing positions. As he explained in a speech given at Harvard University: "If we persist in the practice of Republicans reading only Republican newspapers, listening only to Republican speeches on the radio, attending only Republican political rallies, and mixing socially only with those of congenial views, and if Democrats, Socialists . . . follow suit, we are sowing the seeds of the destruction of our democracy just as surely as if we did not possess this freedom."[1]

He hit upon a scheme of nationally broadcast radio programs, an hour a week, composed of four competing experts and an audience of ordinary citizens, often with remote call-ins from other cities like Philadelphia or Chicago. Launched in 1935, "America's Town Meeting of the Air" was a great success and continued until the mid-1950s on NBC radio and, for a time, on television as well. The transcripts of the discussions were printed up and circulated to thousands of citizens, who were invited to register their views on the same issues.

Denny pioneered many features of the electronic town meeting that are familiar today: the use of ordinary citizens to ask questions of politicians or experts, the use of call-ins from remote cities, the effort to dramatize an issue by a balanced debate among proponents of competing positions. Most important, he had the simple insight that the new electronic medium could be used constructively to engage citizens in thinking about public issues. He aimed at the stimulation of citizen deliberation through an organized conjunction of arguments and counterarguments. Many modern town meetings on television fail to realize such aspirations: they are simply occasions for candidates to answer questions from citizens.

In his lectures Denny was fond of drawing an *R* and a *D* on a blackboard to represent the voters affiliated with each of the two main parties. Then he would add, between them, an *I,* for the Independents, a relatively small number in his time, but comparable to the numbers who support either of the two main parties in our own time. "Here in this middle space is the governing minority of America. If we can educate this minority so that it can know true from false, wise from foolish, it can save America."[2]

"America's Town Meeting of the Air" was organized by the image of the town meeting adapted to the whole nation. It opened with "the Town Crier ringing his bell and calling out in his singsong voice: 'Town Meetin' tonight' and then setting the question for the evening, for example, 'Which Way America—Fascism, Socialism, Communism, or Democracy.'"[3] This was the topic of the first broadcast, and in 1935 it was the question of the day. Proponents of each of the four positions met in fair and open intellectual combat. Their debates were punctuated by questions from the floor, from an audience that had already discussed the issues together before air time.

The broadcast was based on the practices developed by the League for Political Education in its headquarters at Town Hall, New York. Since the 1890s the league had sponsored debates on public matters intended to stimulate more informed citizen discussion. Soon after the success of the "Town Meeting of the Air," the league even changed its name to Town Hall.[4] The broadcasts and the local discussions at Town Hall embodied the same spirit. Both were an effort to bring the serious public debates of the New England town meeting to much larger populations: first, adapted to a big city like New York and second to the entire nation through radio.

Some were skeptical that such an adaptation was even possible. "The desire of a small town to be a city is but half so wistful as the backward glance the metropolis gives to its village," said the *New York Evening News* in its editorial greeting the construction of Town Hall in 1921. "New York's road back to the sociable town meeting is a difficult one. But we can try."

In a large and anonymous society, whether it be New York or the nation as a whole, the effort was fundamentally the same: to restore face-to-face discussion covering opposing sides. Denny contrasted two sorts of politics. The old politics was based on the maxim "Drown out the voices of your opponents if you can." The new type was based on the notion that "The most convincing thing you can do is to let your arguments meet those of your opponents in fair, open combat." Careful moderating and allocation of time is necessary to ensure that competing sides receive a comparable opportunity to state their positions. The result is a "competition of sincerities" in fair and open combat.

The image of the nation drawn by technology into a kind of New England town meeting, the image Denny popularized with "America's Town Meeting of the Air," was later revived by Ross Perot. As early as 1969 he proposed the "electronic town hall" with the ambition of completing the process. He wished to use technology to accomplish the crucial further task performed at actual town meetings—voting. Like Denny, Perot visualized one-hour discussions broadcast on a single issue each week, but he also envisioned millions of viewers following up the broadcasts by sending in cards marked with their voting preferences. The millions of "votes" would then be tabulated by computer, with the results broken down by congressional district so as to inform the people's representatives of their wishes.

As Perot explained the concept:

> Every week or so we would take a single major issue to the people. We would explain it in great detail and then we would get a response from the owners of the country—the people—that could be analyzed by congressional district so that the Congress—no ifs, ands or buts—would know what the people want. Then these boys running around with briefcases representing special interests would be de-horned, to use a Texas term.[5]

When Perot emerged as a presidential candidate in 1992, he pointed out that his proposal was eminently practical. The television network CBS had already broadcast a version of what he had in mind after the president's State of the Union message in January 1991. Anchored by Dan Rather, CBS had called it "America on the Line." After the State of the Union address, CBS tabulated instant reactions from hundreds of thousands of viewers, both to the speech and to current issues in the campaign. About 7 million people tried to call, and around 300,000 succeeded in getting their preferences registered on the air.

Those calling in presented a distorted picture of public opinion, however, compared to CBS's own poll results, which were taken from a representative sample whose responses were announced on the same program. For example, 53 percent of "America on the Line" respondents said they were "worse off" now than a year ago, compared with only 32 percent of the representative sample. Eighteen percent of "America on the Line" respondents reported being in basically the same economic situation as a year ago, while 44 percent of the representative sample reported being the same. Furthermore, the geographical display of respondents pictured in the broadcast suggests that the population of New York State is about twice that of California, when the opposite is the case.[6]

The most obvious problem with this innovation is reminiscent of the *Literary Digest* fiasco in the 1936 election that gave Gallup his initial rise to prominence. Without careful construction of the sample, the sheer number of responses means nothing. "America on the Line" was another SLOP, to use the term for a "self-selected listener opinion poll" coined by Norman Bradburn of the National Opinion Research Center of the University of Chicago. SLOPs do not measure the distribution of opinion because self-selected participation, as we have seen, is skewed toward those who have some motivation to volunteer themselves.

In spite of the *Literary Digest* warning, self-selected polls continue to take many forms. Duds and Suds, a nationwide chain of laundromats, polled about 16,000 of its customers in 1992 on the presidential election and predicted 42 percent for Clinton, 32 percent for Bush and 25 percent for Perot. (They announced that they wished only to encourage candidates to take to the "soap box" and "agitate" the voters.) As the eventual results were 43 percent for Clinton, 38 percent for Bush, and 19 percent for Perot, Duds and Suds did reasonably well. The *My Weekly Reader* poll of almost 700,000 school children, however, was much farther from the mark, predicting a substantial Bush

victory. The most unusual SLOP is probably the KEMB "Cess Poll."
Since 1980 radio station KEMB in Emmetsburgh, Iowa, has given its
listeners a chance to record their opinions of the candidates with requests like: "If you want to vote for George Bush, flush now." The station waits three minutes to calculate the number of flushes based on
the lowered water level at the sewage-treatment plant. Each one-tenth
of a foot represents 113 flushes. In 1992 Ross Perot came in first in this
poll (with Bush second and Clinton third). "If a candidate's campaign
is going down the toilet, it's not necessarily all bad," concluded the
station manager.[7]

The voice of the people can resonate in many ways but those who
listen should be skeptical of self-selected polls. SLOPs are pseudo-rep-
resentations of the people. They have no scientific basis, but once they
are broadcast, their results take on a life of their own. They become
representations of public opinion that are communicated to candidates, commentators, and citizens alike.

After the dust had settled on the presidential election, Perot had an
opportunity to try out his own, full-scale version of the "electronic
town hall." In preparation for his nationally broadcast talk on the issue
of government reform, Perot distributed about 30 million mail-in ballots inside issues of *Reader's Digest* in March 1993. Eventually, his
workers tabulated about 1.3 million responses (a response rate of
roughly 4.3 percent). The resulting sample, which was basically self-
selected, made the results one giant SLOP.

An additional problem with the Perot poll arose from the unbalanced nature of the questions. He asked, for example: "Should laws be
passed to eliminate all possibilities of special interests giving huge
sums of money to candidates?" A *Time*/CNN poll reworded the question so that the alternatives were balanced, with some weight in the
question for each side: "Should laws be passed to prohibit interest
groups from contributing to campaigns, or do groups have a right to
contribute to the candidates they support?" *Time* and CNN tried out
both the Perot versions and the reworded versions on a national rep-

resentative sample (a random half of the sample received one version, half the other). Perot's version of the question received 80 percent "yes" votes, but the balanced version produced only 40 percent in favor of prohibiting contributions, with 55 percent maintaining that groups have a right to contribute to candidates they support. Similar discrepancies emerged from other question wordings. While question wording is an art and not an exact science, such clearly unbalanced questions violate the norms researchers have developed against efforts to manipulate the responses of the public.[8]

These difficulties notwithstanding, Perot's stated goals—to move the debate beyond sound bites and to encourage the public to think about the issues—are laudable. The difficulty is getting the mass public watching a discussion at home to get sufficiently engaged in the issues that it will think them through for more than a top-of-the-head response. As Frank Borman, the former astronaut once hired by Perot to work on the electronic town hall, concluded in an interview with the *New York Times:* "I would not now be in favor of an electronic town hall. . . . I don't think you can take an extremely complex issue and air it completely in a half-hour or hour of television so that people will gain an informed understanding. I don't think you can govern 250 million people with a TV set."[9]

A SLOP does not speak for the people. It only inserts a pseudo-voice in the electronic echo chamber. Better methods are needed to realize—and extend—George Denny's vision of deliberation on the air waves.

TOWARD CIVIC ENGAGEMENT

There are two great moral forces at work in American democracy. One reaches out and the other pulls in. One is centrifugal, one centripetal. Face-to-face deliberation requires getting everyone in the same room, where they can hear all the arguments and come to a decision together. This ideal was articulated by the Founders; it was the rationale for the Federalist boycott of the Rhode Island referendum on the Constitution. It is the force driving the original conception of the electoral college, the party nominating conventions, the New England town meeting, "America's Town Meeting of the Air." It was a force that George Gallup overestimated in his original conception of the public opinion poll because everyone cannot be put, effectively, "in one great room," as he had hoped. Yet it remains an ideal—the ideal of people taking an informed decision after face-to-face discussion together.

The second force, which reaches out, is the desire to widen the range of those who are included. American democracy cannot be limited merely to the propertied, the white, the male; it must also include the poor, the ethnic, and the female. As the suffrage expanded, and as the country expanded, the forces reaching out created mass democracy on a continental scale. But even with this expansion, the values of the other moral force remain with us. Can the explosive forces of expansion and contraction somehow be captured in a single system without the whole dynamic spinning apart?

In our discussion of the Federalists and anti-Federalists, we found four basic principles of democracy bequeathed to us in the American political tradition. From the Federalists we especially learned the values of deliberation and the avoidance of tyranny. From the anti-Federalists we especially learned the values of participation and political equality.

As the franchise has expanded, as more people have been brought into the system, as the society has grown in both population and geography, and as technology and telecommunications have made communication and transportation unimaginably different from what they were in the time of the Founders, the social context for realizing any of these values has changed dramatically. Deliberation requires conditions that will effectively motivate citizens to invest time and effort in information-gathering and face-to-face discussion. In the mass society we have created there are, instead, incentives for rational ignorance and for citizens to report, in opinion polls, a surface impression of sound bites and headlines. Avoiding tyranny of the majority requires a degree of mutual respect and mutual understanding. The occasional passions of a disengaged public may well lay the groundwork for factions adverse to the rights and interests of other citizens (or noncitizens). Participation requires not only the legal opportunity to vote but also a social context that effectively motivates people to vote and to express their views.

Political equality requires not only weighing votes equally in the drawing of districts but some assurance that the process is representative of the entire country. The anti-Federalists raised this issue when they complained that no one could expect a simple farmer to serve in Congress; the anti-Federalists worried that Congress would be peopled solely by lawyers and others with more education. When blacks voted but racial gerrymandering prevented them from gaining representation, the value at stake was also political equality. Although we have achieved a great deal in terms of political equality, when citizens widely support term limits in polls and state referendums, they are saying, in the spirit of the anti-Federalists, that Congress does not strike them as representative. "People like us" are not there.

Furthering *any* of these values requires conditions that reknit the citizenry to the political process: that encourage thoughtful discussion, mutual respect, active participation, and an openness of the process to all groups and strata. We must create public spaces that effectively motivate citizens to become a "public" where realization of these values is possible. We can do this at two levels, the national and the local. The differing social context of the two requires different strategies.

The key to achieving this aspiration, at least at the local level, was uncovered by Alexis de Tocqueville in his celebrated visit to America, when the American Republic was little more than four decades old. The nine months he spent traveling through the country in 1831 and 1832 formed the basis for the two-volume classic, *Democracy in America,* that established him as one of the founders of modern political sociology.

The two characteristics Tocqueville found that astonished him, and from which he drew many shrewd inferences, were the "general equality of conditions" in American society and the propensity of Americans to join "associations" of all sorts. To an aristocratic Frenchman with close ties to the restored French monarchy, the extent of equality in all spheres of American society was striking. But for our purposes, it is his second observation that is crucial, the extent to which ordinary Americans form and join associations:

Americans of all ages, all stations in life, and all types of disposition are forever forming associations. There are not only commercial and industrial associations in which all take part, but others of a thousand different types—religious, moral, serious, futile, very general and very limited, immensely large and very minute. Americans combine to give fêtes, found seminaries, build churches, distribute books, and send missionaries to the antipodes. Hospitals, prisons and schools take shape in that way. Finally, if they want to proclaim a truth or propagate some feeling by the encouragement of a great example, they form an association.[10]

This behavior is different from what Tocqueville would expect in his native France or in Britain. Any new undertaking in France would be led by the government or, in Britain, "by some territorial magnate," but "in the United States, you are sure to find an association" (513). Initiatives come from ordinary people, for every conceivable purpose. Tocqueville paints a picture of ordinary life in America rich in citizen initiative: people joining together to solve common problems. "If some obstacle blocks the public road halting the circulation of traffic, the neighbors at once form a deliberative body; this improvised assembly produces an executive authority which remedies the trouble before anyone has thought of the possibility of some previously constituted authority beyond that of those concerned" (189).

Tocqueville thought that the American propensity to create, and join, associations, when combined with the freedom of the press, permitted a new kind of politics. He seemed amazed by the way ordinary citizens, without special power, status, or wealth, could combine into groups that would seriously grapple with public problems, even on the national stage. He illustrated this novel development with the agitations he observed in 1831 concerning tariffs and free trade. "When the quarrel was most envenomed, an obscure citizen of Massachusetts thought of suggesting through the newspapers that all opponents of the tariff should send deputies to Philadelphia to concert together measures to make trade free" (191). Delegates supporting free trade gathered from all over the United States in an assembly at Philadelphia that "in American fashion styled itself a convention." Tocqueville seemed entranced by the seriousness of the proceedings and the detailed character of the public debate. "The discussions were public, and from the very first day it took on an altogether legislative character; discussion covered the extent of the powers of Congress, theories of free trade, and finally the various provisions of the tariff" (192). There were ten days of deliberation, after which the assembly issued an address to the American people.

What explained this kind of serious political initiative among ordinary citizens? Tocqueville believed that the proliferation of associations and the character of American democracy were inextricably linked. There is only "one country in the world" whose citizens make use "day in and day out" of "unlimited freedom of political association," and there is also only one country whose citizens "have thought of using the right of association continually in civil life, and by this means have come to enjoy all the advantages which civilization can offer." These two countries are one and the same, the United States, which suggests that "there must be some natural, perhaps inevitable connection" (520).

The root of the American propensity for association, Tocqueville believes, is in the relative political equality he found among ordinary American citizens. In a society of equals, individuals must work in combination to do anything. "Associations must take the place of the powerful private persons whom equality of conditions has eliminated" (516). The relative equality of conditions spawns a habit of association that applied both to politics and to all other areas of life.

"As soon as several Americans have conceived a sentiment or an idea that they want to produce before the world," Tocqueville tells us, "they seek each other out, and when found, they unite." In that condition, they are "no longer isolated individuals." They become a power— "when it speaks, men listen" (516).

Tocqueville argues that what Americans learn from politics they take to all the associations of civic life. "It is through political associations," Tocqueville speculates, that "Americans of every station, outlook and age day by day acquire a general taste for associations and get familiar with the way to use the same." The result is a society of joiners and active citizens. "Through [political associations] large numbers see, speak, listen and stimulate each other to carry out all sorts of undertakings in common. Then they carry these conceptions with them into the affairs of civic life and put them to a thousand uses" (524).

Tocqueville's observations on civic life have stimulated a fertile new branch of modern social science, the study of "social capital." The dense network of civic associations Tocqueville discovered created patterns of behavior, norms for how people join together—how they can trust or rely on each other—that can, in themselves, be considered a resource or a form of "capital." Tocqueville calls this "the art of association." Social capital seems to be related to economic development and, more important for our central theme, it seems to facilitate the public connectedness of ordinary citizens. Perhaps the direction of causality is at least as much from civic life to politics, as it is politics to civic life.

In a remarkably inventive study of modern Italy, political scientist Robert Putnam systematically applied the notion of social capital to a great national experiment—the creation of twenty regional governments that began in 1970. The governments were virtually identical, but their social, political, and economic contexts were entirely different. Some of the governments were failures by any economic or political standard, but some were "remarkably successful." They were notable for "creating innovative day care programs and job training centers, promoting investment and economic development, pioneering environmental standards and family clinics—managing the public's business efficiently and satisfying their constituents." What explains such differing results? The government institutions were basically the same; political parties and economic conditions were not themselves decisive factors. Instead, Putnam found that the kind of rich associational life uncovered by Tocqueville in early nineteenth-century America offered the best explanation. "Strong traditions of civic engagement—voter turnout, newspaper readership, membership in choral societies and literary circles, Lions Clubs and soccer clubs—are the hallmarks of a successful regime."[11]

Putnam constructed a Civic Community Index, which included the prevalence of sports and community organizations, the level of newspaper readership, and indexes of voter turnout (under conditions when voting was neither required by law nor connected to patron-client relations). Putnam found a "remarkable concordance between the performance of a regional government and the degree to which social and political life in that region approximates the ideal of a civic community." The "civic" character of a region proved to be a much more powerful predictor of government performance than economic development or any other predictor that Putnam could find.[12] In the high civic areas, the citizens are involved in many kinds of associations: cultural, athletic, literary; they stay connected to public affairs through newspapers and political participation. The role of citizen in such regions is different from that in less civic areas—there is collective engagement with public problems. In the areas of low civic community, politics is characterized by patron-client relations. It is a matter for the "bosses," not the citizens.

Putnam's theme is that the high civic regions, in the north of Italy, have garnered significant social capital, while the low civic regions, concentrated in the south, lack social capital. By social capital he means "features of social organization, such as networks, norms and trust, that facilitate coordination and cooperation for mutual benefit."[13] Social capital is a "public good"—it is a characteristic of the community, and it is available to all the members of that community. The kind of community where trust and mutual cooperation are possible is also the kind of community where governments can function and where the networking and entrepreneurship that facilitate economic development can also flourish. It is a place where citizens have a public life; where public questions meet active, engaged citizens.

Social capital helps facilitate the solution to problems of collective action. We may all benefit from the provision of a public good, but in a large group there is a perverse rationality in my not doing my share to provide that public good. My own actions will have so little effect on whether the public good is provided for everyone, that I can calculate, through narrow self-interest, whether I will be able to acquire the benefits of the public good without making the effort of doing my part. I can be a "free rider" and save the costs of doing my share but still reap the benefits.[14]

The rational ignorance we found afflicting ordinary citizens in modern mass democracy is a symptom of this problem. Why should I invest in acquiring political information to produce the benefits of a better public decision when those benefits, in all reasonable probability, will be provided—or not—regardless of my actions? But citizens in a civic community, one with high social capital, have many reasons to participate in politics together and to stay informed. They are part of a dense network of civic associations, both political and nonpolitical, which provides them lots of reasons to read newspapers, to stay informed, to participate in community activities. They internalize norms that motivate them to participate and to join with others—norms that give them satisfaction regardless of any calculation about the effects of their individual actions. And, as Tocqueville noted, these habits of association, the widespread acceptance of working together, make it far easier for each individual to participate, to combine with others for some cause of mutual interest.

Putnam found astonishing historical stability in the tendency of some communities to have high social capital and others low. The different patterns hold for nearly a millennium. The roots of modern civic-mindedness can be found in the medieval guilds and associations of Bologna and Florence, and in the republican governments of many of the northern Italian city-states. The submissive nonparticipation of the south can be traced back to the autocratic rulers of Sicily in the twelfth and thirteenth centuries.

This stability is intriguing social science, but it is dispiriting as social prescription. "If you know how many choral societies there were in a city in the 1300s," Putnam says, half-seriously, "you can predict how long it will take the government to process a medical insurance claim today."[15] Can a community's stock of social capital be increased, as a matter of either public policy or private initiative? Or is history destiny?

Putnam, and others who have worked in this area, would clearly agree that if we are self-conscious about the unexpected implications of associational life, we can nurture it and employ it as a tool to facilitate both economic development and citizenship.[16]

Ernie Cortes, Jr., offers many examples of what can be done. As director of the Texas Industrial Areas Foundation, or IAF, a statewide network of grassroots organizations, he embraces the concept of social capital, which he terms "a measure of how much collaborative time and energy people have for each other."[17] It is a way of overcoming "the learned helplessness that comes of being disconnected and isolated." His "iron rule" is: "Never do for others what they can do for themselves." The aim is "developing confidence in one's own competence." Training and opportunities for leadership in local grassroots organizations can facilitate the development of social capital and rebuild community.

In a recent talk, he describes the odyssey of one Virginia Ramirez of San Antonio, who was "afraid to speak out because she felt she wasn't educated." But she was "angry at watching a neighbor die because she didn't have enough heat in the winter." Communities Organized for Public Service, or COPS, one of the IAF member organizations, "taught Mrs. Ramirez to tap that anger and forge it into a tool for the renewal of hope in herself and her community." With training, "she learned to speak publicly, to lead actions, to take risks with herself and to guide others." She is now "president of her parish council . . . also a co-chair of COPS." She "leads a team of leaders and pastors engaged in transforming the public hospital system to truly serve the inner city."

Cortes considers Ramirez "extra-ordinary but not unique. The IAF has developed a score-and-ten institutions which have transformed the lives of thousands of persons like her." These organizations can be considered "schools for the development of politics." But not politics in the electoral sense. Rather, it is a "collective action which is initiated by people engaged in public discourse." People have to learn to think, interpret, and deliberate face-to-face. "Politics is about relationships which enable people to disagree, argue, interrupt one another, clarify, confront and negotiate, and through this process of debate and conversation, forge a compromise and a consensus which enables them to act."

Cortes offers an instructive example of how community organizations can be engaged to create social capital. Since 1986 one of the Texas IAF organizations, Allied Communities of Tarrant (ACT), in Fort Worth, began to work closely with Morningside Middle School, a largely African-American public school that "had all but ceased to function as anything other than a holding place for children and adults." In a period of a year and a half, there were over six hundred meetings, many of them individual meetings with the parents of each child. "Parents attended training sessions on how to support their children's study habits. They began to meet more often with their children's teachers individually." Attendance at parent assemblies went way up. An after-school enrichment program staffed by parents was implemented.

The results were dramatic. The children's performance on standardized tests rose from twentieth out of the district's twenty middle schools to third. "The percentage of children failing at least one subject decreased from 50 percent to 6 percent. Police calls fell off to virtually none." The IAF effort activated a community that could support a school with a network of engaged adults working together in support of a common purpose. As a side effect, the program began "changing the culture within families," by calling upon "parents to be parents." It also activated parents to advocate the interests of the school in the broader community. As Tocqueville showed, the norms of community involvement tend to carry over from one activity to another. People learn to work in combination, and the networks created from one association are a resource for other efforts.

The community engagement with the Morningside Middle School helped reproduce for that one school the kind of support structure that sociologist James Coleman and his colleagues discovered distinguished Catholic schools, as opposed to both public and nonparochial private schools. The Coleman study found that community engagement contributed to the success of Catholic schools with otherwise similar students in otherwise similar communities.[18] Yale professor James Comer's work in New Haven similarly rests on engaging the parents and creating a sense of local community to support a school.[19]

These efforts enlist the creation of social capital in support of human capital, that is, education. Creating social capital can also lead to the creation of capital in the more tangible sense of economic resources. Putnam discusses the operation of lending circles and rotating credit associations in places as diverse as Java, Japan, and Bangladesh. "In a typical rotating credit association, each of twenty members might contribute a monthly sum equivalent to one dollar, and each month a different member would receive that month's pot of twenty dollars."[20] This arrangement clearly depends on trust, on the faith that the members will continue to pay after they have received their share.

At first glance, it would seem that a rotating credit association must fail because of collective action problems. After I receive my share, why not stop contributing? But there are two factors in its favor. First, rotating credit associations "select their members with some care."[21] In communities with a dense network of associations, a great deal of information, both from personal contact and reputation, will be available about each potential member. Second, the group relations fostered by regular meetings provide social pressure against defecting, against leaving one's peers holding the bag.

Lending circles, like those fostered by the Women's Self-Employment Project (WSEP), founded in Chicago in 1986, also depend on social pressure in small groups to ensure repayment. In addition, they count on careful, community-based screening of credit risks. But as the *Wall Street Journal* notes about such efforts, they succeed in making loans in communities and to people whom conventional banks shun. In doing so, they also create norms and networks that embody social capital. As the *Journal* describes one WSEP borrower, "Dorothy Wallace would seem a lender's nightmare. Separated from her husband, she is on welfare with her two teenagers. She hasn't held a steady job since 1984. But with WSEP, she has turned into a 'flawless borrower.'" The *Journal* explains how "WSEP depends on other low-income women in Ms. Wallace's 'borrowing circle' to make sure she makes her loan payments on time." The peer-group pressure was successful, not only in Wallace's case, but in all 60 loans the WSEP made over the previous three years. At the time of the *Journal* article, in 1992, they had not experienced a single default.[22] The strategy is not perfect. It is relatively expensive to administer, for instance. But it has the merit of creating social and economic capital in communities that are bereft of both.

We have massive problems in the inner cities, but as we saw in Chapter 1, our public dialogue has become attenuated throughout all strata of society. We have mass democracy with little citizen engagement. And despite the rich associational life documented by Tocqueville, the civic life of Americans has declined precipitously as well. Two-career marriages have led to a decline of leisure. Attendance at Parent-Teacher Association meetings and membership in league bowling are down. The television-politics of mass society encourages citizens to consume sound bites, rather than meet together to solve public problems.

Unless we succeed in rebuilding local communities we may well be in danger of realizing a subtle form of "despotism" to which Tocqueville feared democracies were especially susceptible. While celebrating America's civic community, he described how democratic systems could be vulnerable to a more disquieting form of politics. Contemplating the conditions under which despotism might return to the world he "imagines an innumerable multitude" who are "constantly circling around in pursuit of the petty and banal pleasures with which they glut their souls." What we now call consumerism leads to withdrawal from the community and the loss of public awareness and civic consciousness. "Each one of them, withdrawn into himself, is almost unaware of the fate of the rest. Mankind for him consists in his children and his personal friends." Under such conditions, Tocqueville imagines the state taking over many of the functions he found in associations in America. The government then becomes an "immense protective power" that keeps its citizens in "perpetual childhood." "It likes to see the citizens enjoy themselves, provided that they think of nothing but enjoyment." Such a government "covers the whole of social life with a network of petty, complicated rules." It "hinders, restrains and enervates," until "each nation is no more than a flock of timid and hardworking animals with the government as its shepherd." Because the government "provides for [its citizens'] security" and "facilitates their pleasures" it can also relieve them of the burdens of citizenship in any meaningful sense: "Why should it not relieve them from the trouble of thinking and all the cares of living?" (692).

Tocqueville paints a picture of a democracy with consumers but no citizens, a democracy of individuals but no associations, and a democracy in which people are satisfied but do not think about public issues or shared concerns. Tocqueville's frightening speculation was that such a form of despotism could be "established even under the shadow of the sovereignty of the people" (693). If we can create a democracy of civic engagement at the local level, if we can rebuild social capital in our communities, we may forestall the fate Tocqueville feared.

AIRING THE PEOPLE'S AGENDA

Another of Tocqueville's observations was that "of all countries on earth, it is in America that one finds both the most associations and the most newspapers." In Tocqueville's view, the newspaper served the crucial function of allowing people to combine for common purposes. "Only a newspaper can put the same thought at the same time before a thousand readers." While Tocqueville did not deny that newspapers sometimes stimulated the public to do things that were ill-considered, he offered: "Without newspapers, there would be hardly any common action at all." A newspaper can actuate a common idea among people who are otherwise disconnected. "A newspaper gives publicity to the feeling or idea that had occurred to them all simultaneously but separately. They all at once aim toward that light, and these wondering spirits, long seeking each other in the dark, at last meet and unite." Tocqueville's conclusion was that "hardly any democratic association can carry on without a newspaper" (517–518).

The newspapers Tocqueville found in 1831–1832 were still elite institutions, designed, for the most part, to support a political party or faction, or a specific commercial interest. They were of small circulation and relatively expensive. As it happened, Tocqueville was writing on the eve of a great revolution—the creation of the penny press, which brought newspapers to the masses and divorced them, to a great extent, from particular associations and partisan interests. James Gordon Bennett's *New York Herald,* one of the first mass papers, founded in 1835, proclaimed its independence from any particular group "simply because it is subservient to none of its readers—known to none of its readers—and entirely ignorant who are its readers and who are not."

The later mass newspapers eventually learned to discover who their readers were and what they wanted. In fact, George Gallup first made his reputation with his Gallup Method for surveying readers of newspapers about the features they liked to read and those they did not.[23] In any case, the newspapers Tocqueville found were intimately connected with associations, causes, and interests and seemed, to Tocqueville, to be essential to the kind of civic communities he found so remarkable all over America. But these newspapers were soon supplanted by much larger-circulation papers, many of them more sensational and less serious, based on a different model. Instead of opinion and advocacy, they claimed to provide "news"—facts that could be supported by norms for how facts are supposed to be investigated.

Sociologist Michael Schudson has argued that the development of the mass press and the rise of the ideal of "objectivity" are intimately connected. Newspapers had to disconnect themselves from partisan interests because they came to be sold on street corners, and they therefore needed to appeal to everyone, regardless of politics. News, and the providing of information, came to be the staple of the newspaper. Advocacy waned, except when relegated to the editorial pages or, by the 1920s and 1930s, to the new genre of the political column.[24]

The distinctive thing about the mass circulation paper, in contrast to its elite predecessors, is that it is designed to serve all the people. Admittedly, the demographics vary, as the followers of Gallup's empirical methods soon discovered, but at least the modern mass newspaper lays claim to serving the whole community in the provision of news and information. Objectivity and universal appeal are certainly virtues. But a function that impressed Tocqueville has been lost.

Very simply, Tocqueville saw newspapers as speaking for the people. The newspaper gives "publicity to the feeling or idea" that occurs to people "simultaneously but separately" (518). A newspaper "talks to you briefly each day about the commonweal." But it does so by giv-

ing voice to the views of others. Because of the close connection between associations and newspapers, Tocqueville could say rather
grandly that newspapers "maintain civilization" (517).

Yet as modern newspapers have developed, this function has been
lost. Some voices, segregated onto the editorial pages and into columns,
do speak for the people. But the principal way newspapers have come
to speak for the people has been through polls—public opinion polls
sponsored by and published in newspapers. The findings of polls are
news, and through them the people can speak outside the opinion
pages. However, we have already seen the difficulties in claiming that
opinion polls speak for the people. They offer only a snapshot of opinion when the people may not be thinking deeply or when they may
even have no opinion at all. With the development of modern norms of
reporting, most newspapers view it as their job to present the news,
rather than to facilitate the voice of the people.

Admittedly, opinion polls can be news. But the agenda of questions
is likely to be set by the needs of the news cycle, not, in most cases,
the interests of the public. The picture Tocqueville paints of newspapers discussing the commonweal by giving voice to the ideas of the
public is one that has disappeared from the modern newsroom.

There is, however, a new movement, sometimes called civic or
public journalism, to create a more active and engaged public by self-
consciously giving voice to the people's agenda. This national movement probably got its start in suggestions by influential *Washington
Post* columnist David Broder in January 1990 and a widely read essay
by journalism professor Jay Rosen in 1992. Broder argued that "it is
time for those of us in the world's freest press to become activists, not
on behalf of a particular party or politician, but on behalf of the
process of self-government." This means a new assertiveness "on
the public's right to hear its concerns discussed by the candidates."
We need a respite from "the electronic demagoguery favored by too
many hired-gun consultants. Campaigning must be reconnected to
governmental discussions voters really care about." More generally,

Broder called for an effort to "help reconnect politics and government—what happens in the campaign and what happens afterward in public policy."[25]

Rosen found Broder's words especially notable for saying, in effect, that "the instrument of the press should be employed by *journalists themselves* to alter and improve political debate. Here he crosses into uncharted territory."[26]

Rosen helped give shape to this territory by recounting a recent effort by the *Ledger-Enquirer* of Columbus, Georgia, a small newspaper in a small town southwest of Atlanta. Recognizing that the town faced a host of accumulated economic and social problems, the editors of the paper launched a detailed series about the town's future and the issues they felt the public would need to confront over the long term. They based the series on discussions with experts and on surveys and in-depth interviews with ordinary citizens. What Rosen found instructive about the effort was that when the eight-part series, "Columbus: Beyond 2000," was published in the spring of 1988 it was met, largely, with "silence and inaction."[27]

The series fell into a political vacuum. The issues posed were long-term and difficult—"the sorts of issues governments avoid unless pressured." The people were not engaged or equipped to bring serious focus to such questions, even though public policies affecting their employment and their quality of life were at stake. "The community lacked organization, leadership, debate. It had a government, but it lacked politics—'public politics.'" By "public politics," Rosen means a politics based on citizen engagement and serious dialogue between citizens and leaders.[28]

The newspaper responded by organizing a town meeting and by taking the lead in creating a new civic organization, United Beyond 2000, which organized community task forces staffed by volunteers on specific issues—"recreation needs, child-care issues, race relations and the special problems of teenagers."[29] After a year of continued town meetings, editorials, and further features in the newspaper, the political leadership of the city committed itself to a new strategic plan for the community, which confronted long-term as well as the most obvious and immediate issues.

This example is instructive because it shows how to "reimagine the position of the journalist in politics. Instead of standing outside the political community and reporting on its pathologies, they took up residence within its borders." The journalists had become, in Broder's words, "activists . . . on behalf of the process of self-government."[30] The newspaper stimulated citizen engagement and helped bring it to bear on a public dialogue that affected both leaders and citizens.

The *Ledger-Enquirer* is a Knight-Ridder paper. In 1990 another Knight-Ridder paper, the *Wichita* (Kansas) *Eagle,* began down the same road, in a larger city. By using polling on the issues rather than on the horse race, by extensively reporting on the same issues, by creating opportunities for citizen input on the agenda of discussion, and by cooperating with other local media, the *Eagle* attempted to re-create serious local discussion. The Wichita effort served as a model for an even larger Knight-Ridder project in Charlotte, North Carolina, launched in conjunction with the Poynter Institute.

The *Charlotte Observer* developed a full-scale partnership with WSOC-TV, the local ABC affiliate. It used a poll and a citizens panel of five hundred to formulate a Citizens Agenda. Readers from the Citizens Panel participated face to face in forums that included the major gubernatorial candidates and, in one case, a presidential candidate. The Citizens Agenda guided coverage on six issues for six weeks during the 1992 campaign. It also provided a continuing means for citizens to provide questions to ask the candidates. As a report on the Charlotte project notes, "It's easy to snub a reporter; it's more difficult to duck a direct question from a voter posed by a reporter who intends to print the question whether you answer it or not."[31] Journalists felt "empowered by this alliance with readers." As one concluded: "We weren't just a newspaper anymore, we were the electorate."[32]

The guiding principles of the effort were announced by the editor,

Rich Oppel, at the beginning: "We will seek to distinguish between issues that merely influence an election's outcome, and those of governance that will still be relevant after the election. We will link our coverage to the voter's agenda, and initiate more questions on behalf of voters."[33]

The *Observer*'s commitment to civic journalism continued long after the election. When it ran in-depth stories on crime in an inner-city neighborhood, for instance, "the paper made two remarkable pledges," according to columnist Neal Peirce: "first, to stick with the story for at least a year, and second, to work with the afflicted neighborhoods to find solutions." The *Observer* followed up with town meetings organized on a neighborhood basis, some of which were aired in cooperation with broadcast partners. The *Charlotte Observer* declared in an editorial: "We want to rally the entire community to help these most troubled neighborhoods help themselves."[34] This is a very different stance from that of traditional journalism, in which the journalist reports the "news," but avoids taking an active stance to create events, or to create public dialogue.

By 1994 civic or public journalism took on the character of a movement. Ed Fouhy, producer of the 1988 and 1992 presidential debates, became executive director of the Pew Center for Civic Journalism. In that capacity, he helped nurture and coordinate partnerships around the country in which newspapers, television stations, and radio stations jointly undertook efforts to focus attention on a people's agenda. With eleven major projects around the country, public or civic journalism has moved from tiny Columbus, Georgia, to such cities as Boston, Chicago, Dallas, and San Francisco. Commenting that on most issues, the media "exhibits the attention span of a hummingbird," Fouhy coordinated projects in these cities that aspired to grapple with a citizen's agenda of issues, both during the election and after.

"The People's Voice" project in Boston in 1994 exemplifies the way a newspaper-television-radio collaboration can have a greater impact than any one medium working alone. Along with WBUR-FM and

WBZ-TV, the *Boston Globe* submitted voter questions to each candidate and then featured the voter who suggested the question and published that voter's analysis of the answers from the candidates. Each issue on the citizen's agenda received extensive reports, based on focus groups of citizens as well as input from experts. Publications on each issue were coordinated with radio and television programs broadcast the same day (with times of broadcast published in the newspaper). This effort on the issues was coordinated with the candidate debates. Most remarkable, the first Senate debate between Senator Edward Kennedy and Republican opponent Mitt Romney received a higher rating in the Boston area than the Super Bowl or the O. J. Simpson car chase.[35]

The civic journalism movement has already helped reconceptualize the role of the media in American politics. Instead of standing back from the community, the media situate themselves within the community, attempting to facilitate a serious discussion of shared public problems. Over time, this movement can change campaigns—and change as well the dialogue after campaigns. It can change a community's conception of itself and its conception of its process of self-government.

The press offers us an instrument for seeing the world. But it has often exhibited the blindness of an eye examining itself. Civic journalism allows the press to self-consciously reexamine its role. With civic journalism, it can become not merely an instrument for examining the public but an organ of the public, for examining the problems of the body politic.

If there is a limitation in the practices of civic journalism as developed thus far, it is in the media's reliance on public opinion polls to create the citizens agenda. As Richard Morin, director of polling for the *Washington Post,* notes in evaluating the Charlotte experiments, "Polls can be a mirror or a window. On many issues, survey results merely reflect back what people have superficially absorbed from the media. Instead of peering into the minds of the voters, reporters are sometimes merely seeing themselves in these survey results."[36]

Of course, polls have the advantage over haphazard methods of opinion research—man-in-the-street interviews, self-selected polls, assessments by knowledgeable political operatives—that they are based on scientific samples. They offer a reasonably accurate snapshot of the state of public opinion, such as it may be. But is there some way of preserving this advantage while probing opinions more deeply? Is there some way of encouraging the public to make considered judgments instead of giving snap opinions? A people's agenda based on poll results will sometimes merely reflect the public's impression of what the media have reported. A public dialogue worth listening to should be deliberative as well as representative. Can we start the people *thinking* as we facilitate the people's voice?

THE DELIBERATIVE POLL:
BRINGING DELIBERATION TO DEMOCRACY

"This weekend has proved to me—don't be apathetic, find out about your subject. What I like about it is that we have covered such a wide range of opinions, that the opinion furthest away from me has made me think and strengthened my own opinion." So said Carmel Meredith, a participant in the first nationally televised "deliberative poll," reflecting on a long weekend of intensive discussions with a national random sample of citizens from her country, Great Britain. She is filling out a new questionnaire and contrasting it with the one she filled out four weeks earlier—before she had participated in the process of citizen deliberation. "The questionnaire that I filled in four weeks ago, I might as well rip up now and put in the bin. It was an absolute waste of time—because I didn't know enough about it."

Meredith is one of three hundred randomly selected voters in Great Britain who participated in the world's first nationally televised deliberative poll, in May 1994. Channel 4, one of Britain's four national broadcast networks, made a reality of my proposal for a new institution—the deliberative poll—as a means of giving voice to public views that represent all the people under conditions where they can also think about the issues in question. Since then, the Public Broadcasting Service, MacNeil/Lehrer Productions, the nation's eleven presidential libraries (six Republican and five Democratic), and the University of Texas at Austin have announced a joint plan to conduct the same kind of deliberative poll in the United States at the beginning of the 1996 presidential selection season.

The deliberative poll is unlike any poll or survey ever conducted. Ordinary polls model what the public is thinking, even though the public may not be thinking very much or paying much attention. A deliberative poll attempts to model what the public *would* think, had it a better opportunity to consider the questions at issue.

The idea is simple. Take a national random sample of the electorate and transport those people from all over the country to a single place. Immerse the sample in the issues, with carefully balanced briefing materials, with intensive discussions in small groups, and with the chance to question competing experts and politicians. At the end of several days of working through the issues face to face, poll the participants in detail. The resulting survey offers a representation of the considered judgments of the public—the views the entire country would come to if it had the same experience of behaving more like ideal citizens immersed in the issues for an extended period.

A deliberative poll is not meant to describe or predict public opinion. Rather it prescribes. It has a recommending force: these are the conclusions people would come to, were they better informed on the issues and had the opportunity and motivation to examine those issues seriously. It allows a microcosm of the country to make recommendations to us all after it has had the chance to think through the issues. If such a poll were broadcast before an election or a referendum, it could dramatically affect the outcome.

A deliberative poll takes the two technologies, polling and television, that have given us a superficial form of mass democracy, and harnesses them to a new and constructive purpose—giving voice to the people under conditions where the people can think. Working with WETA, the Washington public broadcasting station, I had proposed a deliberative poll for the beginning of the 1992 primary season to act as a reform for the "invisible primary"—the period when candidates acquire their initial credibility and momentum.[37] However, after an announcement in July 1991, we were unable to raise all the necessary money, and the event was canceled. The Gulf War had delayed serious focus on the coming presidential election, and after the Gulf War, potential sponsors predicted that 1992 would prove an uninteresting election. Over and over I was told, in effect, "What interest will there be in this election when the incumbent has a 90 percent approval rating?"

Disappointed with this result, I went to England on a long-planned sabbatical and managed to persuade the television network Channel 4 and the newspaper the *Independent* to be the first to try out the process on a national basis and on national television.

Roger Jowell, the director of Social and Community Planning Research (SCPR, the independent British research organization that conducted the survey), commented to me, on seeing the entire sample gathered for dinner in one room: "I've selected thousands of national random samples, but I've never *seen* one—no one has." The reason is that by the conventions of survey research, one would never wish to see a sample gathered together. After all, the people might talk to each other: they might discuss the issues and as a result become more informed or change their views. In that sense, they would become unrepresentative of ordinary unreflective public opinion. In my view, they would become representative of something else—representative of the public the people would become if everyone had a comparable opportunity to behave more like ideal citizens and discuss the issues face to face with other voters and with political leaders.

The deliberative poll has not developed in a vacuum. It builds on important work in encouraging citizen deliberation. It also builds on the movement toward public journalism discussed earlier. Most efforts to realize public or civic journalism rely on conventional opinion polling to formulate the "people's agenda," however, and Jay Rosen criticizes the press for having accepted those polls as the appropriate measure of public opinion. He cites the pioneering work of survey researcher Daniel Yankelovich, who distinguishes between "public opinion" and "public judgment." The latter represents what people think, on those occasions when they have had a chance to confront a range of conflicting arguments and conflicting values and arrive, after face-to-face deliberation, at a considered judgment. Public journalism can be thought of as focusing on one single task: "to improve the chances that public opinion will evolve into public judgment."[38]

Yankelovich has spent a productive career as a leading public opinion researcher, conducting sample surveys with the firm that bears his name. But he came to see the superficiality of public opinion and founded, with others, the Public Agenda Foundation, which develops briefing materials designed to facilitate citizen deliberation. The work of the Public Agenda Foundation combined with that of the Kettering Foundation to support the work of a nationwide network of citizen deliberators, the National Issues Forums (NIF). About 3,200 citizen forums around the country are held each year under the auspices of NIF. As David Mathews, the president of the Kettering Foundation, explains, the collaborators in NIF "wanted to develop a different type of public forum, one that would deal with issues from the public's perspective. That meant going beyond technical, ideological and legislative positions to find out how each issue affects what is most valuable to people."[39]

Based on focus groups conducted by Public Agenda, issues are "reframed into three or four options that capture these 'values' or the deeper motivations that are at play. The issue books spell out the consequences of each policy option of what citizens consider most valuable." In thousands of citizen forums around the country, the participants grapple with the pros and cons of each option and see whether, after extensive discussion, they can find any bases for common ground. "The objectives of the forums are to help people to become a public, to develop the skills needed for public politics, to speak in a public voice, and to contribute to defining the public's interests."[40]

The NIF forums facilitate citizen deliberation. But they do so primarily among self-selected groups. Thousands of organizations sponsor them, including "colleges, universities, and secondary schools; libraries and leagues; churches, synagogues, and theological centers; literacy programs and leadership programs; and student associations and senior citizens centers."[41] In all these local settings the discussion is among those who volunteer, agree, or put themselves forward. Hence, the "public voice" of these forums is, inevitably, the voice of that part of the public willing to become engaged in politics, or already engaged. These NIF forums are deliberative, but, given this limitation, they are not representative. Nevertheless, they are an enormously rich and fruitful corrective to conventional opinion polls, which have the opposite problem—they are representative but not deliberative.

Most important, the citizen forums sponsored by NIF and Kettering take us a step closer to a more deliberative and engaged society by providing thousands of citizens with the opportunity and the occasion to think through current issues, to confront trade-offs, and to grapple with the hard choices facing our society. In short, these forums help move a subsection of the country in the direction of public judgment rather than public opinion.

Two representatives of the Kettering Foundation, Bob Kingston and John Doble, helped frame the briefing materials in the British deliberative poll and helped train the moderators for the small group discussion. With similar help, the briefing materials and moderator training for the American project will have the benefit of Kettering and the NIF. In that way, the deliberative process pioneered by NIF in citizen forums around the country can be brought to national television with a statistically representative microcosm to create a public voice that speaks for the people—a public voice that is both representative and deliberative.

We gathered the national random sample for the first deliberative poll, April 15–17, 1994, at the Granada Television Studio in Manchester, England. We attracted participants by paying their expenses, offering them a small honorarium, telling them they would be on national television, and advising them that they would be part of an important experiment in democracy. (We also promised them a chance to visit the sets of the popular prime-time soap opera *Coronation Street* and "Baker Street," where the Sherlock Holmes series is made.)

The sample was selected by SCPR from forty randomly chosen polling districts in forty randomly chosen constituencies around the country. First, we conducted a baseline survey in people's homes, face to face. We needed to find out what people thought before they were invited to come to the weekend. We interviewed 869 citizens, randomly chosen from the electoral register. This survey had a high response rate—74 percent. It gives an excellent picture of the public's attitudes on the issue in question: "Rising Crime: What Can We Do about It?" The survey is highly representative of the entire country in age, class, geographical location, gender, education, and every other important dimension. But this baseline survey was not the deliberative poll. It was only the beginning of the process.

Voters were invited to the Manchester event only after they completed the baseline survey. The three hundred who took up the invitation to come to Manchester for the weekend were, in every important respect, indistinguishable from the 869 who took the baseline survey. In terms of class, education, race, gender, and geography the weekend microcosm was fully as representative of the country as the baseline survey. Even more important was the fact that in their attitudes about crime, and in their political positions generally, the weekend microcosm was just as representative of the country as the baseline survey.

One of the persistent claims of critics was that participants who would take up the invitation for the weekend would be precisely the people who were most interested in the issue, specifically, the people who were most fearful of crime. Instead, the weekend sample turned out to be an almost perfect microcosm. Because this sample matched the baseline sample, it was strikingly representative. About 28 percent of both surveys said crime was "not a worry," exactly 21 percent of both surveys considered it "a big worry," roughly 34 percent of the two thought crime "a bit of a worry," and about 18 percent of both surveys said the issue arose only as "an occasional doubt." The weekend sample was no more and no less fearful of crime than the general public, as measured by our baseline survey.

Another speculation was that primarily men rather than women would accept our invitation. We began to worry about this in focus groups we conducted as we were designing the event. In one focus group, a woman said that she "could never consider coming to an event like this." She explained that she had never spent a weekend away from her husband. But in the very next focus group, another woman said she would "definitely come"—because she'd never spent a weekend away from her husband! In the end, of the 300 participants, 150 were men and 150 were women.

As a starting point on the issue of crime, the weekend sample was an almost perfect representation of the nation gathered together in a single place. The challenge for the experiment was whether the participants would change over the course of the weekend. If a deliberative poll gave results identical to an ordinary poll, it would not be worth investing in such an elaborate project again.

Change, however, was not a worry. The members of the sample began to change from the moment they received our invitation. Knowing that they would be on national television, they began discussing the topic with family and friends, they began to read newspapers and listen to the media with more care, they began reading the briefing materials we sent them. Their views thus immediately became unrepresentative of public opinion in the conventional sense. But those views also became representative in an important new sense. They became representative of the views the entire country would come to if it were populated by persons closer to ideal citizens—people who were motivated to be engaged by the issues and who debated them over an extended period. In short their new, considered judgments offered a representation of what the public would think, if it actually had a better opportunity to think about the issue.

During the deliberative weekend, a woman came up to me and said that during thirty years of marriage, her husband had never read a newspaper but that from the moment he had been invited to this weekend, he had changed. Not only did he read every bit of our briefing materials, but he now read "every newspaper every day." She speculated he would be much more interesting to live with in retirement.

The voters who came to Manchester changed in dramatic and coherent ways. They remained tough on crime (they continued to insist that prison should be "tougher and more unpleasant" and that "the death penalty is the most appropriate sentence" for some crimes), but they offered, by the end, a much more complex appreciation of the problem. Realizing the limits of prison as a tool for dealing with crime, they focused on rehabilitation and on different treatments for first-time juvenile offenders. They also increased their sensitivity to the procedural rights of defendants. The "right to silence"—the right to say nothing when questioned by the police and not have that silence held against one in court—for example, showed a dramatic increase in support. Also, opposition to the police's "cutting corners" to secure a conviction increased significantly. In short, the participants demonstrated a new appreciation for the complexity of the issues, the conflicts of values the issues posed, and the limitations of any one solution. Our participants became far more sophisticated consumers of the competing policy prescriptions. They became, at least on this one issue, more thoughtful and engaged citizens.[42] (See the appendix for a summary of some of the results of the deliberative poll.)

What did the event accomplish? It demonstrated the viability of a different form of opinion polling and, in a sense, a different form of democracy. As we have seen, Americans have long struggled with how to adapt democracy to the large nation-state. Face-to-face democracy cannot be applied to large states. Even in Rhode Island, the anti-Federalists could not gather everyone together to hear all the arguments on either side. It was for this reason that the Federalists boycotted the referendum on the U.S. Constitution and said that the only appropriate method for making a decision was the elected state convention. A *representation* of the people, in the form of those elected to go to the convention, would be able to hear all the competing arguments and make an informed decision.

But recall the persistent anti-Federalist worry that no *elected* representation would be representative. Ordinary people like them—farmers, laborers, people without a great deal of education—would tend to get left out. The lawyers and judges and wealthy elite of the day would make the decisions. The elected microcosm, in other words, would not be a genuine microcosm—and might not consider or understand *their* interests.

Democracy, even in the elitist sense of the Founders, was only revived by the notion of elected representation. But another form of representation lay hidden in the dust of history. It was employed by the legislative commissions, citizens' juries and the Council in ancient Athens (the crucial body that set the agenda for meetings of the citizen Assembly). This other method was selection by lot or random sampling. In one sense the use of random sampling in politics was revived by opinion polling. After all, what is a random sample, at bottom, but a lottery? But in the ancient Greek form, and in the form employed in the deliberative poll, opinions are taken not from isolated citizens but from citizens meeting together, deliberating on common problems. These polls represent the considered judgments of the polity, not the top-of-the-head reactions of isolated citizens. Institutions that speak for the people need to be both representative and deliberative. The ancient Greek innovation was a random sample of citizens who deliberated together and in that way realized both values. And this is the form I propose to adapt to the television age.

If this new—and very old—form of democracy were employed in

a general election, at the beginning of the primary season, or before a referendum, then the recommending force of the public's considered judgments, broadcast on national television, might well make a difference to the outcome. Recall Samuel Popkin's argument that voters are inclined to follow cues as arbitrary as President Ford's choking on a tamale in San Antonio.[43] Surely, the cues formed from an elaborate deliberative process should be worth paying attention to. When broadcast on national television and disseminated in the press, the deliberative poll can affect the public's conclusions, but it can also affect the way that public frames and understands issues. If televised deliberative polls succeed in communicating the deliberative process, they can help transform the public agenda to the agenda of an engaged public — to an agenda citizens will care about, and be attracted by, because it will be framed in terms that speak to their concerns in ordinary life.

Channel 4 has already announced a deliberative poll for the next British General Election. The American project, at the beginning of the presidential selection season, can be expected to have a major effect on candidates and issues. During the invisible primary the national broadcasting of the considered judgments of the entire country, in microcosm, could provide for a more thoughtful and representative way of launching the primary season and launching the debate. In 1992 only 12 percent of Democrats and 8 percent of Republicans in the relevant states participated in the primary process. As we have seen, the arbitrariness in the ordering of the primaries increases the influence of tiny, self-selected electorates in determining the outcome for the rest of us. Furthermore, given the increasing domination of television as the key medium of public discourse, the primary process has become a duel of attack ads and sound bites fighting for the attention of an inattentive public. The deliberative poll would insert a rational dialogue at the start, one that represents the entire country in one room, under conditions where it can think through the issues. Given the increasingly front-loaded character of the primary calendar, approximately 70 percent of the delegates will be selected in seven weeks in 1996: the entire country has been turned into one giant television battleground, one huge California primary, if you will. The new and constructive use of television offered by the deliberative poll will give us a thoughtful prelude to the accelerated process to follow. The deliberative poll may, in fact, be the one time when the country will be able to pause, take a deep breath, and think through the issues. The rest of the primary season will then proceed with the speed of a shrinking sound bite.

Most ambitiously, the deliberative poll can be thought of as an actual sample from a hypothetical society—the deliberative and engaged society we do not have. Ideally, we should get everyone thinking and discussing the issues. But as we have seen the forces of rational ignorance are powerful. Yet although we cannot get everyone actively engaged under most conditions, through the deliberative poll we can do the experiment and get the microcosm engaged—and then broadcast the results to everyone else. Citizens in the microcosm are not subject to rational ignorance. Instead of one insignificant vote in millions each of them has an important role to play in a nationally televised event. With true engagement and attention from the microcosm this representation of the public's judgment becomes a voice worth listening to.

One of the key decisions we made in planning the British deliberative poll sheds light on the experiment's aspirations, both in Britain and in the United States. The problem was the seemingly simple issue of where in the schedule to place the small-group discussions. We struggled with two different models of how these discussions serve the deliberative process. One is by *absorption,* the other is by *activation.* In one model the respondents *absorb* information from competing experts, mull that information over in small groups, and form their conclusions. On this model the participants would spend a great deal of time listening to competing presentations of relevant factual materials and then they would process those materials in small group discussions.

In the second model, we attempt to do something far more ambitious. There, the small group discussions come first, before participants have any contact with experts or politicians. On this strategy, we facilitate the citizens' melding into groups first, identifying their key concerns first, establishing rapport among themselves first, setting the agenda of the questions and concerns they wish to raise first—and only then put them together with the competing experts and competing politicians. The second model, instead of absorbing its agenda from the experts, energizes a public voice coming *from* the citizens so that it can speak *to* the elites. This strategy was followed in the Manchester experiment, and it set an example for how we hope to conduct future deliberative polls.

At the National Issues Convention, scheduled for mid-January 1996, we intend to identify, far in advance, several key issue areas, based on analyses of such standard public opinion research as polls and focus groups. We shall use standard public opinion research because we are interested in beginning where the public begins. We must select issues that speak to the people's concerns and that facilitate posing the problems in terms they can understand. Working with the Kettering Foundation and the Public Agenda Foundation, we shall adapt briefing materials appropriate for ordinary citizens as an initial background on the issues. Those briefings will be reviewed for both balance and accuracy by a distinguished bipartisan committee chaired by former Democratic Congresswoman Barbara Jordan and former Republican Congressman Bill Frenzel. Candidates who wish to provide materials on these issues will be invited to do so. We expect that the citizens invited to participate will prepare seriously for the event. Knowing that they will be on national television, and knowing that the issues are important, they are likely to read the materials, discuss the issues with friends and family, and pay more attention to the media. From the moment they are invited, they begin to become unrepresentative of mass opinion as it is. But they begin to become representative of our ideal public.

The logic is very simple. If we take a microcosm of the entire country and subject it to a certain experience, and if the microcosm (behaving in the way we would like ideal citizens to behave in seriously deliberating about the issues) then comes to different conclusions about those issues, our inference is simply that if, somehow, the entire country were subjected to the same experience as the microcosm, then hypothetically the entire country would also come to similar conclusions.

Of course, it is unlikely the entire country ever would approximate the experiences of a deliberative poll. Even when there is an intense debate, it may well be dominated by attack ads and misleading sound bites. But the point is that if, somehow, the public were enabled to behave more like ideal citizens, then the deliberative poll offers a representation of what the conclusions might look like. That representation should have a prescriptive value. It is an opportunity for the country, in microcosm, to make recommendations to itself through television under conditions where it can arrive at considered judgments.

Earlier I emphasized four democratic values—deliberation, non-tyranny, political equality, and participation. I noted that efforts to fully realize all four have usually been unsuccessful. In particular, the move toward mass democracy—a move realized by increasing participation and political equality—has had a cost in deliberation. By transferring the effective locus of many decisions to the mass public, the system is far less deliberative than it would have been had those decisions been left in the hands of elites—elected representatives and party leaders. The deliberative poll, however, offers a *representation* of a democracy that meets all four conditions. With a deliberative atmosphere of mutual respect, tyranny of the majority is unlikely. When all the citizens are effectively motivated to think through the issues, when each citizen's views count equally, and when every member of the microcosm participates, the other three values are realized as well. Fully realizing those values throughout the entire society may be hypothetical. But we can see, in microcosm, what deliberation, political equality, participation and non-tyranny would look like.

Suppose, hypothetically, that the new institution of deliberative polling somehow became as accepted a part of our public life as, say, conventional polling is today. Deliberative polling at the state and local level need not be unusual or expensive. Transportation is a key component of the expense on the national level, and local deliberative polls would not face such a hurdle.

The experience of serious citizen deliberation seems to have a galvanizing effect on the participant's interest in public affairs. So far the evidence for this proposition has been largely anecdotal, but we hope to study this phenomenon systematically in follow-ups with participants in the British project. Suppose, for the sake of argument, that there is a *continuing* effect. In the same way that the citizen mentioned earlier was galvanized to read "every newspaper every day," we might imagine that he continues to be a far more engaged citizen—discussing public issues with others, being more aware of the media, and becoming more likely to participate in public or civic affairs. If deliberative polls ever became a staple of public life, we would end up with a society of more seriously engaged citizens—one which was not just a *representation* of how all four democratic values could be achieved but rather an *embodiment* of their achievement. Just as the apparatus of selection by lot in ancient Athens involved so many citizens, so often, that it seems to have galvanized an active citizenry, it is not inconceivable that selection by lot for deliberative polls could, someday, have the same effect on our own country.

It is not inconceivable, but it is, admittedly, unlikely. Such a flourishing of a new institution is clearly utopian, even as a matter of aspiration. But the image helps clarify an ideal—a picture of the reconstructed role of citizen, not just on television but in actual life. At a minimum, the deliberative poll can articulate the considered judgments of an informed citizenry and broadcast those conclusions to the nation. It provides a different, and more thoughtful, public voice. Other innovations and other institutions would have to be relied on if we are to create a seriously engaged mass citizenry as a routine part of our national life.

When George Gallup articulated his vision for the original opinion poll, it was to "restore" the democracy of the New England town meeting to the large nation-state. He thought the poll would put everyone in one enormous, metaphorical room, where they could think through the issues. Radio and newspapers would communicate the views of elites and the views of citizens would be communicated back by the opinion poll. But the room, the "one great room" of the entire country connected by the media, was too large—so large that no one was listening. People tuned out because the large room fostered rational ignorance. And, apart from national crises, they often tune out, as we can see from nearly half a century of public opinion research since.

The deliberative poll, however, attempts to fulfill Gallup's initial aspiration to somehow adapt the New England town meeting, the image of serious face-to-face democracy, to the large nation-state. In doing so it purports to overcome rational ignorance and represent us all. But even if this new departure succeeds, it is not a panacea. Remember that in our discussion of *Magic Town* there were two distinctive outcomes—first, the people felt a responsibility to form considered judgments because they spoke for the nation; second, they helped create an engaged community, where they could work together in a spirit of mutual sacrifice for public causes. In effect, they created social capital.

Without functioning communities of engaged citizens, television programs, by themselves, have limited impact. They may suffer the fate of the initial series published by the *Ledger-Enquirer,* which fell on deaf ears because the community was not prepared for such a dialogue. Television can be a catalyst, but it cannot, by itself, change the country. It can only begin to change the discussion.

To make a democracy that works, we need citizens who are engaged, communities that function, and media that speak *for* us as well as *about* us. If we pay attention to the conditions under which citizens become reconnected to political life, we can create a public worthy of public opinion—and public judgment. It would indeed be "magic town" if we brought such a spirit to the entire country.

APPENDIX

The First Deliberative Poll:
Summary of Results

At this writing, I am at work with my academic colleagues in the British deliberative poll—Robert Luskin (University of Texas) and Roger Jowell and Rebecca Gray (both of SCPR) on a systematic analysis of what happened in the Manchester deliberative poll of 1994. We have joint publications in preparation. In the meantime, this informal summary may provide a useful picture of the experiment.

REPRESENTATIVENESS

The independent London research institute SCPR selected a national random sample from forty randomly chosen polling districts in forty randomly chosen constituencies in Great Britain. Of this sample, 869 people responded to a baseline survey, with a response rate of 74 percent. Three hundred people participated in the Manchester experiment, held April 15–17, 1994. On every demographic and attitudinal dimension, the 300 are indistinguishable from the 869.

On the issue of whether crime is a worry, for example, note this comparison of the baseline survey and the weekend sample:

Crime	Baseline survey	Weekend sample
No worry	28%	27%
A big worry	22%	21%
A bit of a worry	34%	35%
An occasional doubt	16%	17%

Furthermore, on every important question about what should be done about crime, the weekend sample presented a near-perfect microcosm of the baseline sample. To take just two key ways of reducing crime, "reducing unemployment" and giving "stiffer sentences generally," the following results were discovered:

	Very effective	Effective	Neither effective nor ineffective	Not very effective	Not at all effective
Reduce unemployment					
Total	43	38	7	9	3
Weekend	44	38	11	4	3
Stiffer sentences generally					
Total	52	26	13	6	3
Weekend	51	27	15	5	2

RESULTS: BEFORE AND AFTER

Key changes in the After survey (compared to the baseline survey for the three hundred):

1. The respondents show an increased sense of the limitations of prison as a tool for fighting crime.
   •Agree that "send more offenders to prison" is an effective way of preventing crime: down from 57 to 38 percent (**).

•Agree that "the courts should send fewer people to prison": up from 29 to 44 percent (**).

•Agree that "stiffer sentences generally" is an effective way of fighting crime: down from 78 to 65 percent (**).

2. The respondents show an increased willingness to employ alternatives to prison, both for juveniles and for offenders more generally.

•Strongly against sending first-time burglar, aged 16, to an ordinary prison: up from 33 to 50 percent (**).

•Agree to a strict warning while leaving the juvenile to the parents to sort out: up from 49 to 63 percent (**).

•Favor compulsory training and counseling for criminals who are not a big threat to society: up from 66 to 75 percent (**).

•"If the government had to choose, it should concentrate more on punishing criminals or it should concentrate more on trying to reform criminals": punish, down from 54 to 47 percent (*).

3. The responses show an increased sensitivity to procedural rights of defendants.

•Strongly disagree that the police should sometimes be able to "bend the rules" to get a conviction: up from 37 to 46 percent (**).

•Believe it is "worse to convict an innocent person" than "to let a guilty person go free": up from 62 to 70 percent (**).

•Agree that "suspects should have the right to remain silent under police questioning": up from 36 to 50 percent (**).

•Agree that "if a suspect remains silent under police questioning this should count against them in court": down from 58 to 41 percent (**).

•Agree that "a confession made during police questioning should not on its own be enough to convict someone": up from 67 to 78 percent (**).

4. In spite of the increased sensitivity to procedural rights, the respondents remain tough on crime. They have *not* been turned into "lib-

erals": they remain impatient with the impediments to getting a conviction.

•Agree that "the rules in court should be *less* on the side of the accused": up from 42 to 52 percent (**).

•Agree that "the death penalty is the most appropriate sentence" for some crimes: unchanged at 68 percent.

•Agree that "prison life should be made tougher and more unpleasant": unchanged at 71 percent.

•Agree that "Prison life is too soft": virtually unchanged at 75 from 73 percent.

5. The respondents also show movement toward traditional values.

•Agree that "teach children the difference between right and wrong" is a very effective way to help prevent crime: up from 66 to 77 percent (**).

•Agree that "parents spending more time with their children" is a very effective way to help prevent crime: up from 53 to 66 percent (**).

•Agree that "less violence and crime on television" is an effective way of preventing crime: up from 67 to 74 percent (**).

6. Respondents show increased knowledge on issue of crime.

•"Britain has a larger prison population than any other country in Western Europe": correct (true), up from 50 to 80 percent (**).

•"Britain has more people serving life sentences than the rest of the European Community put together": correct (true), up from 20 to 58 percent (**).

•"Possible to be tried by a jury in a local magistrate's court": correct (false), up from 58 to 68 percent (**).

Note that all the changes above are *net change*. Many more respondents changed than is indicated by these figures because on many questions change in one direction was canceled out by change in the other. For example, on "the courts should treat suspects as innocent until proved guilty" there was virtually no net change, but only half (46 percent) gave the same answer both times.

Note: The symbol (*) means that the difference between the before and after survey is significant at the 5 percent level in a two-tailed test, and (**) that the difference is significant at 1 percent level.

NOTES

Chapter 1
Introduction

1. There are well-known difficulties with any claim that a particular town or district mirrors the nation. See, for example, Edward R. Tufte and Richard A. Sun, "Are there Bellwether Electoral Districts?" *Public Opinion Quarterly* 39:1 (Spring, 1975): 1–18. Even Tufte and Sun, who see only limited predictive power in bellwether districts, identify 12 counties out of 3,100 that averaged within 2.5 points of the national electoral swing during the period they studied, 1916–1968. As befits the probable location of Grandview, 11 of the 12 are in either north central Illinois or northern Indiana.

2. See Bruce A. Ackerman, "Constitutional Law/Constitutional Politics," *Yale Law Journal* 99 (1989): 453–547, for similar observations.

3. I would like to thank Walter Dean Burnham for his generous help with this discussion of third parties.

4. David Mathews, president of the Kettering Foundation, has made this point eloquently.

5. *The* Republic *of Plato,* trans. Francis MacDonald Cornford (New York: Oxford University Press, 1982), p. 227.

6. See "Fair Exchange," *Newsday,* April 6, 1993, p. 46.

7. I am indebted to Tom Seung for his study of Plato's *Laws.* See T. K. Seung, *Rediscovering Plato* (Lanham, Md.: Rowman and Littlefield, 1996).

8. I take this phrase from Alexander Hamilton, in *Federalist* no. 71. See Hamilton, James Madison, John Jay, *The Federalist Papers,* ed. Clinton Rossiter (New York: New American Library, 1961), p. 432.

9. V. O. Key, Jr. (with Milton Cummings), *The Responsible Electorate* (Cambridge, Mass.: Harvard University Press, 1966), p. 2.

Chapter 2
Who Speaks for the People?

1. Alexander Hamilton, James Madison, John Jay, *The Federalist Papers*, ed. Clinton Rossiter (New York: New American Library, 1961), p. 33. All further references to the *Federalist* will be to this edition and will be cited in text by issue number. See also Herbert J. Storing, ed., *The Complete Anti-Federalist*. 7 vols. (Chicago: University of Chicago Press, 1981), vol. 1, p. 3.

2. Mogens Herman Hansen, *The Athenian Democracy in the Age of Demosthenes* (Oxford: Basil Blackwell, 1991), p. 55.

3. *The* Politics *of Aristotle,* ed. and trans. Ernest Barker (New York: Oxford University Press, 1958), 1326b, pp. 291–292.

4. As we shall see, "electronic town meetings" will tend to be neither representative nor deliberative. Even the deliberative poll (see Chapter 5) does not fulfill mass participation.

5. We now know that there were some 750 city-states in ancient Greece, many of them democracies. But the detailed historical record has restricted most discussion of ancient Greek democracy to Athens.

6. See Clinton Rossiter in Hamilton, Madison, Jay, *Federalist Papers,* p. 100.

7. Anthony Downs, *An Economic Theory of Democracy* (New York: Harper and Row, 1956).

8. See Samuel Popkin, *The Reasoning Voter* (Chicago: University of Chicago Press, 1991).

9. At least, that is the term some modern scholars have used. See Jon Elster, *Solomonic Judgments: Studies in the Limitations of Rationality* (Cambridge: Cambridge University Press, 1989), pp. 85–86. The principal source for the Spartan system is Plutarch's *Lycurgus.* See *Plutarch on Sparta,* trans. Richard A. Talbert (London: Penguin Books, 1988). A detailed description of the Shout can be found on pp. 38–39.

10. Michael Wines, "Washington Really Is in Touch. We're the Problem," *New York Times,* October 16, 1994, sect. 4, p. 1.

11. By engaged citizens, I mean those with incentives to participate in our ideal of democratic discussion.

12. Quoted in "Ears Glued to Phones," *Roll Call,* February 1, 1993.

13. "Rhode Island's Assembly Refuses to Call a Convention and Submits the Constitution Directly to the People," in Bernard Bailyn, ed., *The Debate on the Constitution: Federalist and Antifederalist Speeches, Articles and Letters during the Struggle over Ratification,* Part 2 (New York: Library of America, 1993), pp. 270–275; quotations from p. 274.

14. "The Freemen of Providence Submit Eight Reasons for Calling a Convention, March 26, 1788," in Bailyn, *Debate,* pp. 277–278.

15. North Carolina also turned down the Constitution in a state convention, but after Madison gave notice that he would press Congress for a Bill of Rights, a second

convention, convened at Fayetteville, approved the Constitution in November 1789. See Michael Lienesch, "North Carolina: Preserving Rights," in Michael Allen Gillespie and Michael Lienesch, eds., *Ratifying the Constitution* (Lawrence: University Press of Kansas, 1989), pp. 343–367, esp. pp. 362–364.

16. See John P. Kaminsky, "Rhode Island: Protecting State Interests," in *Ratifying the Constitution*, pp. 368–390.

17. Samuel Greene Arnold, *History of the State of Rhode Island and Providence Plantations,* vol. 1: 1636–1700 (New York: Appleton, 1859), p. 102.

18. Ibid., p. 203.

19. "Speech to the Electors of Bristol on Being Elected (Nov. 1774)" in *The Political Philosophy of Edmund Burke,* ed. Iain Hampsher-Monk (London: Longman, 1987).

20. Ibid., p. 110.

21. *Roll Call,* February 1, 1993.

22. Quoted in Storing, *Complete Anti-Federalist,* vol. 2, p. 379.

23. William C. Adams, "As New Hampshire Goes . . . ," in Gary R. Orren and Nelson W. Polsby, eds., *Media and Momentum: The New Hampshire Primary and Nomination Politics* (Chatham, N.J.: Chatham House, 1987), pp. 42–59. See esp. p. 42.

24. See Adams, pp. 44–45.

25. See, for example, Jürgen Habermas, "A Reply to My Critics," in John B. Thompson and David Held, eds., *Habermas: Critical Debates* (Cambridge, Mass: MIT Press, 1982), pp. 218–283.

26. See the creative proposals by Norman Ornstein and Thomas Mann in *Renewing Congress* (Washington, D.C.: American Enterprise Institute, 1992).

27. Blendon is quoted in "Health-Care Polls Perplex Congress; Debate Leaves the Public Confused," *Chicago Tribune,* May 16, 1994, p. N 7. See also Kaiser Health Reform Project: Kaiser/Harvard/PSRA *Survey of Public Knowledge II* (March 1994), Henry J. Kaiser Family Foundation, Menlo Park, California. A good example of efforts to present Americans with polls that offer trade offs is the work of the Americans Talk Issues Foundation. See Alan F. Kay, Frederick T. Steeper, Hazel Henderson, Celinda Lake, and David J. Hansen, "What the American People Want in the Federal Budget" (Washington, D.C.: Americans Talk Issues Foundation, 1992), Survey 18.

28. See Joseph Tussman, *Obligation and the Body Politic* (New York: Oxford University Press, 1960).

29. Judith N. Shklar, *American Citizenship: The Quest for Inclusion* (Cambridge, Mass.: Harvard University Press, 1991), pp. 25–26.

30. Of course, the United States is unusual for putting the entire burden of registration on the individual citizen. Some have argued that the appropriate comparison is the percentage of registered (rather than eligible) voters who vote. See David Glass, Peveril Squire, and Raymond Wolfinger, "Voter Turnout: An International Comparison," *Public Opinion* 6:6 (December–January 1984): 49–55.

31. See, most notably, Raymond Wolfinger and Steven Rosenstone, *Who Votes?* (New Haven: Yale University Press, 1980).

32. Frances Fox Piven and Richard A. Cloward, *Why Americans Don't Vote* (New York: Pantheon, 1989), p. 12.

33. Maureen Dowd, "Americans Like GOP Agenda but Split on How to Reach Goals," *New York Times,* December 15, 1994, p. 1.

34. Newt Gingrich, interviewed on CNN, January 4, 1994, before the opening session of the new Congress.

35. I am grateful to my colleague Walter Dean Burnham for sharing these perceptive observations with me and for giving me permission to refer to these data.

36. See for example, Steven J. Rosenstone and John Mark Hansen, *Mobilization, Participation and Democracy in America* (New York: Macmillan, 1993), p. 42.

37. *Roll Call,* February 1, 1993.

38. Stephen Engelberg, "A New Breed of Hired Hands Cultivates Grass Roots Anger," *New York Times,* March 17, 1993, sect. A, p. 1.

39. Samuel Butler, *Hudibras,* quoted in Edmund S. Morgan, *Inventing the People: The Rise of Popular Sovereignty in England and America* (New York: Norton, 1988), p. 227.

40. Joseph A. Schumpeter, *Capitalism, Socialism and Democracy* (New York: Harper and Row, 1942), pp. 242–243.

41. I take the term *Constitutional Moment* from Bruce Ackerman. See his *We the People: Foundations* (Cambridge, Mass.: Harvard University Press, 1990).

42. Daniel A. Farber and Suzanna Sherry, *A History of the American Constitution* (Saint Paul, Minn.: West Publishing, 1990), pp. 16–17.

43. For a useful overview see Elmer E. Cornwell, Jr., *Presidential Leadership of Public Opinion* (Bloomington: Indiana University Press, 1965), chap. 2.

44. Push polls are a misuse of survey research for negative campaigning. In a push poll, a misleading characterization of a candidate or position is communicated to the public through widespread telephone pollings.

45. Robert A. Dahl, *A Preface to Democratic Theory* (Chicago: University of Chicago Press, 1956), p. 6. Throughout this book, I am greatly influenced by Dahl's landmark discussion.

46. For a more extended development of this notion of majority tyranny, see my *Tyranny and Legitimacy* (Baltimore: Johns Hopkins University Press, 1979).

47. I wrote this after Proposition 187 in California was passed, in 1994. This proposition, among other things, denies secondary education to the children of illegal immigrants.

48. Hansen, *Athenian Democracy,* pp. 313–314. No citizen could repeat as "president of Athens" after serving for a single day (certainly a most severe version of term limits).

49. See Stanley Crawford, *Mayordomo: Chronicle of an Acequia in Northern New Mexico* (Albuquerque: University of New Mexico Press, 1988).

50. Ralph Waldo Emerson, "Historical Discourse at Concord," quoted in Jane J. Mansbridge, *Beyond Adversary Democracy* (New York: Basic, 1980), p. 126.

51. See Mansbridge, ibid., pp. 130–132.

52. Max Farrand, ed., *The Records of the Federal Convention of 1787*. Rev. ed. 4 vols. (New Haven: Yale University Press, 1966), vol. 1, p. 50.

53. I am indebted to Jane J. Mansbridge for this observation.

54. Stanley Elkins and Eric McKitrick, *The Age of Federalism: The Early American Republic, 1788–1800* (New York: Oxford, 1993), p. 22. Hamilton was more elitist than Madison, and among the Founders there were advocates for greater popular participation. James Wilson of Pennsylvania, for example, argued for popular election of the Senate as well as of the president. He was, in other words, against the Founders' initial strategy of successive filtrations.

55. Quoted in Douglass Adair, *Fame and the Founding Fathers,* ed. Trevor Colbourn (New York: Norton, 1974), pp. 99–100.

56. James Madison, "Vices of the Political System of United States," in Robert A. Rutland et al., eds., *The Papers of James Madison* (Chicago: University of Chicago Press, 1975), p. 357.

57. Storing, *Complete Anti-Federalist,* vol. 2, pp. 380–381.

58. Ibid., vol. 2, p. 249.

59. Ibid., vol. 3, p. 158.

60. Ibid., vol. 1, p. 61.

61. See for example, Storing, ibid., vol. 4, p. 275: "Annual election is the basis of responsibility" ("A Colombian Patriot"), vol. 3, p. 159 (the Pennsylvania Minority objecting to "long terms in office"); and vol. 1, p. 17.

62. James S. Fishkin, *Justice, Equal Opportunity, and the Family* (New Haven: Yale University Press, 1983).

Chapter 3
How "Public Opinion" Became the Voice of the People

1. Shlomo Slonim, "The Electoral College at Philadelphia: The Evolution of an Ad Hoc Congress for the Selection of the President," *Journal of American History* 73 (June 1986): 35–59; quotation is from p. 57.

2. Henry Jones Ford, *The Rise and Growth of American Politics* (New York: Macmillan, 1898), pp. 213–214.

3. In terms of the values identified earlier, political equality and participation together are furthered by gains in popular control.

4. Neal R. Peirce and Lawrence D. Longley, *The People's President: The Electoral College in American History and the Direct Vote Alternative*. Rev. ed. (New Haven: Yale University Press, 1981), p. 49.

5. In spite of this image of deliberation at work, it is worth pointing out that the first party conventions nominated candidates by acclamation. The first national party

convention to have a real nomination struggle was the 1844 Democratic Convention, which unexpectedly nominated James K. Polk. I would like to thank Dean Burnham for this point.

6. Cited in William H. Riker, "The Senate and American Federalism" *American Political Science Review* 49 (June 1995): 452–469. This section has benefited greatly from Riker's insightful article.

7. Congressional Record, vol. 47, p. 1743 (June 7, 1911), cited in Riker, "Senate and American Federalism," p. 467.

8. William Bennett Munro, " 'Such was the Man'—the Bryce that I Knew," in Robert Brooks, ed., *Bryce's* American Commonwealth: *Fiftieth Anniversary* (New York: Macmillan, 1939), pp. 204–235. The quotations are from p. 206.

9. James Bryce, *The American Commonwealth,* vol. 2 (New York: Macmillan, 1933), pp. 267, 268. Further references will be to this edition and will be cited parenthetically in the text.

10. For an excellent assessment, particularly of the influence of elites via the media, see John R. Zaller, *The Nature and Origins of Mass Opinion* (Cambridge: Cambridge University Press, 1992).

11. George Gallup, *The Pulse of Democracy: The Public Opinion Poll and How It Works* (1940; New York: Greenwood, 1968), p. 18; George Gallup, "Public Opinion in a Democracy." The Stafford Little Lectures. (Princeton: Princeton University Extension Fund, 1939), p. 6.

12. Gallup, "Public Opinion," pp. 6–7. "The successful candidate is frequently tempted to regard his election as a blanket endorsement of his entire program, although in point of fact, this may not express the real intentions of his supporters": Gallup, *Pulse of Democracy,* p. 18.

13. Gallup began with quota sampling and did not move to random sampling until after the debacle of the 1948 election, where he predicted Dewey over Truman.

14. Gallup, "Public Opinion," 14–15.

15. Ibid., p. 15.

16. Ibid.

17. John Brehm, *The Phantom Respondents: Opinion Surveys and Political Representation* (Ann Arbor: University of Michigan Press, 1993), p. 3.

18. Eugene Hartley, *Problems in Prejudice* (New York: Columbia University Press, 1946), pp. 10–12.

19. See George F. Bishop, Robert W. Oldendick, Alfred J. Tuchfarber and Stephen E. Bennett, "Pseudo-Opinions on Public Affairs," *Public Opinion Quarterly* 44 (1980): 198–208.

20. Philip E. Converse, "The Nature of Belief Systems in Mass Publics," in David E. Apter, ed., *Ideology and Discontent* (New York: Free Press, 1964), p. 245.

21. Philip E. Converse, "Attitudes and Non-Attitudes: Continuation of a Dialogue," in Edward R. Tufte, ed., *The Quantitative Analysis of Social Problems* (Reading, Mass.: Addison-Wesley, 1970), p. 171.

22. Ibid., p. 176.

23. W. Russell Neuman, *The Paradox of Mass Politics: Knowledge and Opinion and the American Electorate* (Cambridge, Mass.: Harvard University Press, 1986), p. 23.

24. See Michael W. Traugott, "The Impact of Media Polls on the Public," in Thomas E. Mann and Gary R. Orren, ed., *Media Polls in American Politics* (Washington, D.C.: Brookings Institution, 1992), pp. 125–149.

25. See Shanto Iyengar and Donald Kinder, *News that Matters: Television and American Opinion* (Chicago: University of Chicago Press, 1987).

26. See "Nine Days in America," *Economist* (London), May 8, 1976, p. 11.

27. Richard Morin, "What Informed Public Opinion? A Survey Trick Points Out the Hazards Facing Those Who Take the Nation's Pulse," *Washington Post National Weekly Edition,* April 10–16, 1995.

28. See Benjamin I. Page and Robert Y. Shapiro, *The Rational Public: Fifty Years of Trends in Americans' Policy Preferences* (Chicago: University of Chicago Press, 1992), pp. 17–23.

29. "Higher Learning in the Nation's Service." Carnegie Foundation for the Advancement of Teaching (Washington, D.C., 1981).

30. The phrase comes from James Russell Lowell in 1888 and is taken by Michael Kammen for the title of his book *A Machine That Would Go of Itself* (New York: Random House, 1986). Lowell is cited on p. 18.

31. See Thomas Grey, "Do We Have a Written Constitution?" *Stanford Law Review* 27 (1975): 703–718.

32. Principles can be distinguished from rules in terms of the kind of interpretation they require. For an illuminating discussion, see Ronald Dworkin, *Law's Empire* (Cambridge, Mass: Harvard University Press, 1986), chap. 1.

33. The phrase "derived from public opinion" comes from Samuel Williams, *The Natural and Civil History of Vermont* (Walpole, N.H.: Isaiah Thomas and David Carlisle, 1794), quoted in Gordon Wood, *The Creation of the American Republic, 1776–1787* (New York: Norton, 1969), p. 612.

34. Quoted in Wood, *Creation of the American Republic,* p. 533.

35. Max Farrand, ed., *The Records of the Federal Convention of 1787.* Rev. ed. 4 vols. (New Haven: Yale University Press, 1966), vol. 2, p. 476.

36. Wood, *Creation of the American Republic,* p. 342.

37. A Pennsylvania legislator, cited by William Nelson, *The Fourteenth Amendment: From Political Principle to Judicial Doctrine* (Cambridge, Mass: Harvard University Press, 1988), p. 94.

38. Bruce A. Ackerman, "The Storrs Lectures: Discovering the Constitution," *Yale Law Journal* 93 (1984): 1013–1072; see p. 1065.

39. See Bruce A. Ackerman, *We the People: Foundations* (Cambridge, Mass: Harvard University Press, 1991).

Chapter 4
Who Are the People?

1. Chilton Williamson, *American Suffrage: From Property to Democracy 1760–1860* (Princeton: Princeton University Press, 1960).

2. Quoted in Williamson, *American Suffrage,* p. 11.

3. Anthony Trollope, *Phineas Finn,* vol. 1 (London: Oxford University Press, 1949), p. 297.

4. Ibid., p. 312.

5. Quoted in Williamson, *American Suffrage,* p. 147.

6. Williamson, ibid., p. 117.

7. See Edmund Morgan, *American Slavery, American Freedom* (New York: Norton, 1975), p. 4.

8. Merrill D. Peterson, ed., *The Portable Thomas Jefferson* (New York: Penguin Books, 1975), p. 238.

9. Quoted in Willard Sterne Randall, *Thomas Jefferson: A Life* (New York: H. Holt, 1993), p. 277.

10. Peterson, *Portable Thomas Jefferson,* p. 188.

11. See Noble E. Cunningham, Jr., *The Life of Thomas Jefferson: In Pursuit of Reason* (New York: Ballantine, 1987), pp. 12–13.

12. Peterson, *Portable Thomas Jefferson,* p. 215.

13. Philip S. Foner, ed., *The Life and Writings of Frederick Douglass,* vol. 5 (New York: International Publishers, 1975), p. 401. My discussion of Frederick Douglass has been greatly enriched by Shelley Fisher Fishkin and Carla L. Peterson, "We Hold These Truths to be Self-Evident: The Rhetoric of Frederick Douglass's Journalism," in Eric J. Sundquist, ed., *Frederick Douglass: New Literary and Historical Essays* (Cambridge: Cambridge University Press, 1990), pp. 189–204.

14. Foner, *Life and Writings of Douglass,* pp. 401–403.

15. Ibid., pp. 403, 405. Douglass singles out one such July 4 speech, in particular, by a Mr. Choate.

16. "What to the Slave Is the Fourth of July?" Appendix in Frederick Douglass, *My Bondage and My Freedom* (New York: Arno, 1968), pp. 441–445; quotation is from pp. 443–444.

17. Ibid., p. 444.

18. Foner, *Life and Writings of Douglass,* p. 407.

19. Paul M. Angle, introduction, in Angle, ed., *The Complete Lincoln-Douglas Debates of 1858.* (Chicago: University of Chicago Press, 1991), pp. xxxviii–xxxix. All further references to the debates will be to this edition and will be cited parenthetically in the text.

20. Foner, *Life and Writings of Douglass,* pp. 407, 409.

21. Quoted in Garry Wills, *Inventing America: Jefferson's Declaration of Independence* (Garden City, N.Y.: Doubleday, 1978), p. xvi.

22. Also quoted by Douglass in Foner, *Life and Writings of Douglass,* pp. 409–410.

23. Harry V. Jaffa, *Crisis of the House Divided: An Interpretation of the Issues of the Lincoln-Douglas Debates* (1959; Seattle: University of Washington Press, 1973), p. 42.

24. Ibid., p. 25.

25. The Buchanan Democrats also received 5,071 votes, denying the Lincoln Republicans a majority. See Angle, *Lincoln-Douglas Debates,* p. xliv.

26. Michael W. McConnell, "The Forgotten Constitutional Moment," *Constitutional Commentary* 11 (Winter 1994): 115–144; quotation is from p. 129.

27. Booker T. Washington, quoted in W. E. B. du Bois, *The Souls of Black Folk,* in his *Writings:* The Suppression of the African Slave-Trade; The Souls of Black Folk; Dusk of Dawn; *Essays and Articles from* The Crisis, ed. Nathan Huggins (New York: Library of America, 1986), p. 393.

28. W. E. B. Du Bois, *Souls of Black Folk,* in ibid., 393.

29. Ibid., 404, 398–399.

30. Ibid., pp. 424, 425, 360, 364–365.

31. Ibid., p. 438.

32. Ibid., p. 404.

33. Alexis de Tocqueville, *Democracy in America,* ed. J. P. Mayer, trans. George Lawrence (Garden City, N.Y.: Anchor Doubleday, 1969), pp. 252–253n.

34. Charles W. Chesnutt, *Disfranchisement,* in Ulysses Lee, ed., *The Negro Problem: A Series of Articles by American Negroes of To-Day* (1903; New York: Arno, 1969), p. 84. Further references are to this edition and are cited parenthetically in the text.

35. Abigail M. Thernstrom, *Whose Votes Count? Affirmative Action and Minority Voting Rights* (Cambridge, Mass: Harvard University Press, 1987), p. 2.

36. See Chesnutt, *Disfranchisement,* p. 117.

37. Thernstrom, *Whose Votes?* p. 2.

38. Gerald N. Rosenberg, *The Hollow Hope: Can Courts Bring About Social Change?* (Chicago: University of Chicago Press, 1991), pp. 60–61.

39. Mark E. Rush, *Does Redistricting Make a Difference? Partisan Representation and Electoral Behavior* (Baltimore: Johns Hopkins University Press, 1993), p. 2. More generally on issues of racial redistricting, see the excellent paper by Mark E. Rush, "*Shaw v. Reno* and the Curious Evolution of Voting Rights Jurisprudence," presented at the Southwestern Political Science Association, San Antonio, Texas, March 1994.

40. Frank R. Parker, "Racial Gerrymandering and Legislative Reapportionment," in Chandler Davidson, ed., *Minority Vote Dilution* (Washington, D.C.: Howard University Press, 1984), pp. 85–117.

41. Parker, "Racial Gerrymandering," pp. 85–117; see esp. p. 87.

42. Ibid., p. 89.

43. 247 F. Supp. 96 (M.S. Ala. 1965); discussed in Parker, ibid., pp. 92–96.

44. Parker, ibid., pp. 96–99.

45. See Armand Derfner, "Vote Dilution and the Voting Rights Act Amendments of 1982," in Davidson, *Minority Vote Dilution,* pp. 145–166.

46. Thernstrom, *Whose Votes?* p. 3.

47. Chandler Davidson, "Minority Vote Dilution: An Overview," in Davidson, *Minority Vote Dilution,* pp. 8–9.

48. *Shaw v. Reno,* 113 S. Ct. 2816, 2826–2827 (1993).

49. See Daniel Polsby and Robert Popper, "Ugly: An Inquiry into the Problem of Racial Gerrymandering under the Voting Rights Act," *Michigan Law Review* 92 (December 1993), p. 652.

50. See Ronald Rogowski, "Representation in Political Theory and Law," *Ethics* 91 (April 1981): 395–430.

51. Quoted in June Sochen, *Herstory: A Record of the American Woman's Past* (Palo Alto, Calif.: Mayfield, 1982), p. 62.

52. Margaret Forster, *Significant Sisters: The Grassroots of Active Feminism* (New York: Oxford University Press, 1984), pp. 213–215.

53. Elizabeth Cady Stanton, "Speech to the Anniversary of the Anti-Slavery Society" (1860), in Ellen Carol DuBois, ed., *The Elizabeth Cady Stanton-Susan B. Anthony Reader* (Boston: Northeastern University Press, 1992), p. 81.

54. Stanton, *History of Woman's Suffrage,* vol. 1, p. 419, cited in DuBois, *Reader,* p. 11.

55. Forster, *Significant Sisters,* p. 209.

56. "The Declaration of Sentiments," in *The Concise History of Woman Suffrage,* ed. Paul Buhle and Mary Jo Buhle (Urbana: University of Illinois Press, 1979), p. 96.

57. Stanton, "Address Delivered at Seneca Falls," July 19, 1848, cited in DuBois, *Reader,* p. 32.

58. "Declaration of Sentiments," 94–95.

59. Ibid., p. 96.

60. Stanton, "Address of Welcome to the International Council of Women" March 25, 1888, cited in DuBois, *Reader,* p. 215.

61. Susan B. Anthony, cited in DuBois, *Reader,* p. 154.

62. Mike Cassidy, "Statue? Statue? Oh, You Mean that Fool Statue," *San Jose Mercury News,* January 30, 1994, p. 1B. I am grateful to Denny Crimmins for suggesting this example.

63. Quoted in Joe Rodriquez, "Serpent Wars," *San Jose Mercury News,* September 19, 1993, p. 7C.

64. Cassidy, "Statue? Statue?"

65. Anna Julia Cooper, *A Voice from the South* (New York: Oxford University Press, 1988), p. 163.

66. Ibid., pp. 163–164.

67. Ibid., p. 165.

68. See, for example, two classic studies: Samuel A. Stouffer, *Communism, Con-*

formity and Civil Liberties (New York: Doubleday, 1955), and James Prothro and C. W. Grigg, "Fundamental Principles of Democracy," *Journal of Politics* 22 (1960): 276–294.

69. See Michael Kammen, *A Machine That Would Go of Itself* (New York: Random House, 1986), where this is a central theme.

70. David Cannadine, "The British Monarchy, c. 1820–1977," in Eric Hobsbaum and Terence Ranger, eds., *The Invention of Tradition* (Cambridge: Cambridge University Press, 1983), pp. 142–143.

71. Ibid., p. 142.

72. See the classic discussion in Arthur M. Schlesinger, Jr., *The Imperial Presidency* (Boston: Houghton Mifflin, 1973), which focuses on foreign policy but also has more general implications

73. 310 U.S. 586, 596 (1940); 310 U.S. 586, 599 (1940); 310 U.S. 586, 600 (1940).

74. Justice Jackson, "Board of Education v. Barnette," reprinted in Robert Paul Wolff, ed., *Political Man and Social Man* (New York: Random House, 1966), p. 182.

75. Ibid., p. 189.

76. Ibid., p. 188.

Chapter 5
Giving the People Voice

1. Quoted in Harry A. Overstreet and Bonaro W. Overstreet, *Town Meeting Comes to Town* (New York: Harper and Row, 1938), p. 19.

2. Ibid., p. 25.

3. Overstreet and Overstreet, *Town Meeting*, p. 15.

4. Overstreet and Overstreet, ibid., p. 113.

5. Quoted in Neal R. Peirce, "Electronic Town Halls? Right On, Ross," *National Journal,* June 6, 1992, p. 1367.

6. See James S. Fishkin, "Beyond Teledemocracy: America on the Line," *Responsive Community* 2: 3 (1992): 13–19.

7. *All Things Considered,* National Public Radio, November 2, 1992, transcript.

8. See Elizabeth Kolbert, "Perot to Hold His Own Vote, but This Time on Television," *New York Times,* March 20, 1993.

9. Michael Kelly, "The 1992 Campaign: Third-Party Candidate; Perot's Vision: Consensus by Computer," *New York Times,* June 6, 1992, sect. 1, p. 1.

10. Alexis de Tocqueville, *Democracy in America,* ed. J. P. Mayer, trans. George Lawrence (Garden City, N.Y.: Anchor Doubleday, 1969), p. 513. Further references are to this edition and are cited parenthetically in the text.

11. Robert D. Putnam, "The Prosperous Community: Social Capital and Public Affairs," *American Prospect* 13 (Spring 1993), p. 36.

12. Referendum voting is not required by law in Italy, and preference voting, where one indicates both party preference and the choice of a particular candidate, is

taken as an indicator of patron-client relations. See Robert D. Putnam, *Making Democracy Work: Civic Traditions in Modern Italy* (Princeton: Princeton University Press, 1993), pp. 91–97; quote on p. 98.

13. Putnam, "Prosperous Community," 35–36.

14. The classic discussion is Mancur Olson, *The Logic of Collective Action* (New York: Schocken, 1968).

15. Quoted in David R. Boldt, "The Civic Virtue of Singing Together," *Baltimore Sun*, September 7, 1994, p. 15A.

16. See James S. Coleman, Thomas Hoffer, and Sally Kilgore, *High School Achievement: Public, Catholic, and Private Schools Compared* (New York: Basic, 1982). See also the discussion of Ernie Cortes, below.

17. The quotations in this section from Ernie Cortes, Jr., are from his talk "Reweaving the Fabric: The Iron Rule and the IAF Strategy for Power and Politics," in Henry G. Cisneros, ed., *Interwoven Destinies: Cities and the Nation* (New York: Norton, 1993); I have also relied on his "Politics of Social Capital," *Texas Observer*, January 29, 1993, pp. 16–17, and personal discussions.

18. Coleman, Hoffer, and Kilgore, *High School Achievement*.

19. See James P. Comer, *School Power: Implications of an Intervention Project* (New York: Free Press, 1980).

20. Putnam, *Making Democracy Work*, p. 167.

21. Ibid., p. 168.

22. David Wessel, "Two Unusual Lenders Show How 'Bad Risks' Can Be Good Business," *Wall Street Journal,* June 23, 1992.

23. David W. Moore, *The Superpollsters: How to Measure and Manipulate Public Opinion in America* (New York: Four Walls Eight Windows, 1992), p. 45.

24. Michael Schudson, *Discovering the News: A Social History of American Newspapers* (New York: Basic, 1978).

25. David Broder, "Democracy and the Press," *Washington Post,* January 3, 1990, p. A 15.

26. Jay Rosen, "Politics, Vision, and the Press: Toward a Public Agenda for Journalism," in *The New News and the Old News: The Press and Politics in the 1990s* (New York: Twentieth Century Fund, 1990), pp. 7–8.

27. Ibid., p. 12.

28. Ibid.

29. Ibid., p. 13.

30. Ibid., p. 14.

31. Edward D. Miller, "The Charlotte Project: Helping Citizens Take Back Democracy," *The Poynter Papers,* no. 4 (St. Petersburg, Fla.: Poynter Institute, 1994), p. 45.

32. Ibid., p. 87.

33. Ibid., p. 21.

34. Neal R. Peirce, "Charlotte Launches Unconventional Crime Crusade," *Times-Picayune* (New Orleans), July 5, 1994, p. B 7.

35. The Kennedy-Romney debate of October 25, 1994, received a rating of 42.3 percent of the television households, as compared to 38.7 percent for the 1994 Super Bowl or 41.7 percent for the O. J. Simpson car chase. See Frederic M. Biddle, "Senate Race Debate Proves a Winner in TV Ratings," *Boston Globe,* October 27, 1994.

36. Richard Morin, "Newspapers Ask Their Readers What's Important," *Charlotte Observer* (North Carolina), June 14, 1994.

37. Jeff Kampelman and I developed the initial proposal, based on my article "The Case for a National Caucus: Taking Democracy Seriously," *Atlantic Monthly,* August 1988, pp. 16–18.

38. Rosen, "Politics, Vision, and the Press," p. 26.

39. David Mathews, *Politics for People: Finding a Responsible Public Voice* (Urbana: University of Illinois Press, 1994), p. 108.

40. Ibid., p. 108.

41. Ibid., p. 109.

42. For a more detailed account, see my "Britain Experiments with the Deliberative Poll," *Public Perspective* 5:5 (1994): 27–29, and the accompanying article by Norman Webb, "What, Really, Should We Think about 'The Deliberative Poll?'" in the same issue.

43. See the discussion in chapter 3: "Is there a Rational Public?" above.

INDEX